The Roadie Wife
Finding My Way, Book II
A MEMOIR

by Bethany Luchetta

Cover photo credit: Bethany Luchetta

© Cover Design by Pink Olive Design **www.pinkolivedesign.com**

Dedication

For Garrett, Jordan & Nathan.
For my siblings & cousins; their children
and children's children.

Chapters

1.   What lies beneath
2.   Couples Therapy
3.   Regrets
4.   Homeopathic Therapy
5.   Dirty Girl
6.   Mistaken identity
7.   Kids
8.   Unborn
9.   More loss
10. Control
11. Hypnotherapy
12. The snip
13. Legacy of Brokenness
14. Pregnancy
15. Best Birth
16. Livvy Lou
17. Work
18. Bonding
19. Sleeping fear
20. Intimacy
21. Old patterns
22. The pendulum
23. Enmeshment
24. Fawning
25. Decisions
26. Moving House

27.   Intruder

28.   Sexual Healing Journey

29.   Spinning out

30.   Inner healing

31.   Life skills

32.   Inherited family trauma

33.   Progress

34.   Business coach

35.   My sign

36.   Soul care

37.   Demons

38.   Zombies

39.   The problem of pain

40.   Deracination

41.   Voices

42.   Uncomfortable

43.   Fort Wayne

44.   Breaking the curses

45.   Forgiveness

46.   Deliverance

Epilogue

Deliverance Recap

Special Thanks

Previously in The Roadie Wife

Bethany loses her first husband, David, whom she loved dearly, via divorce and later his death. But between the divorce and his death, although still in love with David, she marries Vince, a touring sound engineer with two daughters. Her new marriage is threatened by an emotional affair, depression, and death. Through the life of a roadie wife, Bethany has adventures with her best friend, Victoria; finds comfort from her pastor, Cathy; and is challenged to face her past and her family legacy. Pick up a copy of The Roadie Wife at your local bookstore or online for the full story before reading The Roadie Wife, Finding My Way, Book II.

Chapter 1

WHAT LIES BENEATH

August 2012, I was at lunch with my grandmother. Nana sat across from me at a little chicken place down from my real estate office. I often walked there for lunch because the fresh air and sunlight would lighten my mood.

Nana was telling her usual stories — how so-and-so was doing, about her doctors' appointments and her doctors' families, her hairdresser's life, and the dentist's handsome son. I was married to Vince now, but she still would point out handsome available men to me.

Suddenly, as though she were merely talking about the weather, she dropped a bomb on me. Nana connects dots to trauma in her memory as though following a map in her mind. Maybe we all do this, and I just notice it with her. She moves down the tracks in her mind to an unknown destination if a trigger word is said or particular memories are jogged. She says something that seems out of the blue to everyone else, but it makes sense to her, and she continues on as if her story made a perfect connection. And then, without emotion, she returns to talking about the weather.

"Aunt Alpha had it hard, you know. She was my favorite sister-in-law. It was so sad that her mother died when she was eight and then her dad raped her. He would allow men from his poker parties to have their way with her, too. She was barren, you know. Never could have kids. That poor girl. My girls just loved her. She was so sweet. Those Jones boys, they all had something wrong with them. How's your chicken, honey?"

"The chicken is fine," I replied.

The chicken may have been fine, but I was not. The room was spinning, and I was lost in some other dimension. I had never heard this story about Aunt Alpha's dad and his poker buddies, and yet the words "Your father sent me in here" were words that had echoed over and over in my own ears for years. I felt terror rising in my chest and began to disassociate from the present reality of having lunch with Nana. I had to turn off my senses.

But that wasn't my life. It hadn't happened to me. I was not raped. My father had not sent friends into my room at night.

Yet somehow that statement, those words — "Your father sent me in here"— I had heard them before. They were the words I heard in my head almost every time I had sex with someone. When the perverted thought first began, I thought it was just me. But it felt like torture. They were words I could not shut off. How in the world was I connected to my Aunt Alpha in this way? What was happening to me?

I felt dizzy and sick and confused. Was I experiencing some out-of-body thing? Did Aunt Alpha pass down her memories to me? Was this even possible? I was reliving something out of the horror movie What Lies Beneath.

Nana was still talking, but I wasn't listening. Much like the grown-ups talking in the Peanuts cartoon, all I heard was a dull "wah whoa wah, wah whoa wah" as I drifted into my own mind. I needed to know more about this information that vibrated in the core of my being. I needed to know what was happening to me.

After lunch I went back to my desk and Googled "shared experiences or feelings or thoughts or memories from other people in your family." What do you even Google for something like this?

After a while I stumbled upon something that struck a chord — the term cognitive resonance. I had heard of cognitive dissonance in psychology classes during my undergraduate work, but never cognitive resonance.

I was losing myself in the woo-woo. Hold on: Is this like déjà vu, but not mine? I was reading that cognitive resonance can be similar to déjà vu — something so familiar you'd swear it happened to you, but it actually happened to a relative instead.

I was beginning to wonder if I was crazy. Was this junk science? But no matter how hard I tried to snap back into reality, I couldn't shake those words. The ones I used to think were just in my mind alone went from tormenting me to upsetting me now in a different way.

Luckily my husband, Vince, had just found a therapist for the marriage crisis we were experiencing at the time, and I would be able to ask his professional opinion on what felt like a new level of insanity for me. But until I was able to see the therapist, I spent every free moment doing online research. Then I ordered books on the subject and began reading what little resources I could find. All the information I was finding felt strange, but familiar. Oddly, things started to make more sense than any explanation I had previously created for myself.

When I did get to see Aaron, our therapist, I asked him for his take on what had happened at lunch with Nana. I searched his eyes for a reaction and peeked over his clipboard to see if he was writing "CRAZY LADY" in my file. But he replied as if we were having a normal conversation. It came as no surprise to him that I could be connected to my aunt at a deeper level.

So, if humans are connected by DNA, and we can share experiences in some paranormal way, what does that mean! This wasn't just an "experience"! I didn't share the actual experience. A memory that wasn't mine? It was too odd.

I kept trying to convince myself it was just a fluke. I told myself that my memories were mine; they didn't belong to someone else. That's the definition of a memory anyway, right? Maybe I should settle back into what I had previously concluded from my having tormenting sexual thoughts — I was innately dirty and perverted. I had already owned these traits as part of who I was.

Chapter 2

COUPLES THERAPY

Vince and I had just returned from celebrating our anniversary in Hawaii in October 2012 when he began a slow crumble since he had just stopped drinking - cold turkey - in order to wade through our personal struggles. It seemed like he was now in full detox. I call this season the "snowball-down-the-mountain" season. It seemed like he was finally releasing some pent-up anger and guilt, and not just from our disconnected marriage but from his former one, too, and perhaps further back. Most of our interactions over the coming months were less marital and more business — we each had "business" to attend to, and it wasn't with each other.

We both were going down our own paths of unloading junk from the trunk. I began asking God how to find healing and wholeness in the fissured parts of my soul. I was clearly distant from myself. Why was I afraid of those parts of myself? I felt the answer — because it was dark in there.

Aaron, our therapist, advised us during one of our first meetings that our problems were not marriage problems, they were people problems. He told me that I would be better off in the long run, whether our marriage made it or not, to focus on my own brokenness and pain rather than on "what Vince did to me." I wrote a note to myself about Aaron's advice in my journal: "Life is messy. Humanity is imperfect. Get used to it." Truer words have never been spoken.

I did not do a flawless job following Aaron's advice. I would occasionally end up drilling Vince with a myriad of questions about his emotional affair, all repeating the same theme: Did he have sex with her — or anyone? Did he get physical in any way? Did he love her? How long had the relationship been going on — and why?

Vince got frustrated — at himself for losing my trust and in wondering if I would ever grow through the pain. Honestly, I wondered the same. I am not an expert on trusting myself, or trusting others, or really knowing when other people are lying. (Truth be told, I think everyone is lying all the time.) But I was doing my best and left the door open to hear his answers, prepared for new information that may have not been forthright at first.

I asked myself, how would I feel if he had gotten physical with another lady while I was with him? What would I do if he did admit to falling in love and yet decided our marriage was his priority? Could I be okay with that?

Did it really matter what he answered? I wasn't sure. Maybe it would have changed my mind about staying in the marriage; maybe it wouldn't have. With all the questions asked, he never got defensive. Frustrated, yes. Maybe I was hoping for more pushback, a fight. He had been broken open, though. Exposed. I felt he had nothing left to hide. Nothing he knew about, anyway.

Actually, this would be our new journey: What did we not know about ourselves and each other?

As Vince and I shut ourselves down to each other, we each made two commitments: one, to work on our own personal growth and health, and, two, we would try to not worry about the other person's journey — how they were doing or what they were doing. We would stay married and communicate if either of us changed our mind about those commitments.

Aaron added, along with my not focusing on "what Vince did to me," that I was not to worry about Vince's feelings. Sounds harsh. But I needed that permission.

What I didn't know at the time was that not worrying about Vince's feelings would mean I would have only mine to worry about. And I soon found out that I had no idea what mine were. I had no idea what to do when I wasn't busy worrying about someone else. That stumped me. I didn't like the sudden attention I was giving my own internal state. It made my skin crawl. How did I get here? This was my constant question. I hated seeing glimpses of why and how, so I would shrug and stuff them. Dots were connecting in front of me, but I was in denial.

Vince and I saw Aaron together only a handful of times. Then Aaron said we each needed our own therapy. Week after week I saw Aaron, for months on end. I knew Aaron hadn't told me to focus just on myself for my sake alone. It was for Vince's sake, too. Vince needed to focus on himself. Aaron prepared Vince to answer any questions I asked without defensiveness. Vince's responsibility was to focus on his own growth and not worry about my response to his journey. I had to ask: Who is Bethany in all of this, and how does she feel?

Chapter 3

REGRETS

There is a theory that opposites attract. Maybe. But maybe it's not actually a rule for romantic relationships. It's more like you marry someone at the same level of emotional and mental health, wherever you may be on the continuum. You are attracted to what makes you comfortable, what is familiar. I began to wonder if I was actually searching for deeper answers through the men I chose. David, my first husband, and now Vince (not to mention all the other guys in my life) — hadn't they all been the same in many ways? Similar levels of dysfunction. Similar wounding. Pain needing resolution.

In the moments of the moving pieces of David's death and Vince's betrayal -- David died in June 2012; I found out about Vince's emotional affair in July of that year --I was content with the answers I was getting from Vince. I was uncomfortable but moving in a new direction. It was painful to face so many unknowns. We humans have thick skulls, don't we? We have to wait until "the shit hits the fan" and have the whole pile of shit weighing down on us before we decide it's too much to carry.

So many people were asking what had happened to David. Unfortunately, when David's mom told me the details of his passing, I ended up misspeaking about the incident. It wasn't on purpose; I just misunderstood what she had explained. I was also too naïve to know what certain terminology meant. Since I was the one making a lot of the calls to let friends know of his passing, several people ended up with misinformation on how he died because of me. I would spend months cleaning up the mess of this and living in regret over how I had made it appear. More to learn — again.

The details of David's death were sensitive. David did not overdose. David never did any hard drugs, to my knowledge, or to the knowledge of anyone who knew him. I also believe David was not trying to kill himself. But in those moments of calling people, I am sure I made it sound like it was some type of overdose or suicide. I hadn't intended to convey that message and am still sorry about my miscommunication. I think it created a mess and some awkwardness for his family. Talk about insult to injury — or would it be injury to insult? Either way, I was behind it, and I shamed myself constantly for being ignorant.

I was candid about how David had passed away while he was attending a bachelor party. The reports showed that he had weed and alcohol in his system. That's not a huge shocker. But his cause of death was shocking — psychedelic mushrooms. It was so shocking that the district attorney ended up involved in the case because it is very rare that mushrooms would end in death without foul play.

David's friends, and family, knew there hadn't been any wrongdoing. The district attorney seized tons of David's stuff from his apartment to try and trace the mushroom dealer. Many people were ready to go to battle with the district attorney, if necessary, in order to protect David's friends from being incriminated regarding his death at the bachelor party.

Sadly, David wasn't just an attendee at the bachelor party; he was a groomsman. It was a tragedy for the wedding. It's sad enough when someone young dies without the extra burden of accusations and all the effects on the wedding at hand.

In the weeks following David's passing, his mother, Tina, told me about all the calls he had been making to people before he died — to friends, family, to me. People kept reporting to her about the call that they had had with David. Several said the calls were heartfelt and lengthy. But not mine. I never answered the phone. We conjectured the calls were his goodbyes.

Tina wondered if David had known something was fatally wrong with him physically. She told me about the recent health scare he had had and his trips to the doctor. David, like many guys, hated going to the doctor for anything. The fact that he was actually concerned enough to go to the doctor and to tell his mom about it pointed to a possible medical concern that may have been exacerbated by whatever he had consumed at the party.

I kicked myself for not answering the calls David made to me in the months before his passing. I tormented myself with agony and regret. I didn't answer the calls because of my own issues. I loved David but was trying to move on in my new marriage, and I couldn't keep pining after him, or talk to him about the mess unraveling with Vince.

Amid all this uncertainty, one thing was certain — I would blame myself for David's demise for a long time. I realize I am not that powerful, but it sure felt like it then. I felt like I was an evil villain who had power to save him and didn't. Was our split the cause of his misery? Did I try hard enough? I guess that is called remorse.

If my theory on how people attract each other is true, it means I was as equally broken as David. I couldn't just say David got off course suddenly. We both had been off course for a long time and hadn't known it.

I cried a lot throughout my counseling. Depression and grief swallowed me up. I pulled away from relationships, especially from Vince and anyone close, and drank alone a lot. A lot of the time my marriage and future felt hopeless. But, somehow, I could also see how the story might be different if I just kept looking for answers. I am not sure where that hope came from. But I was thankful for it.

Chapter 4

HOMEOPATHIC THERAPY

My lupus diagnosis was pending as Thanksgiving approached. I was still waiting to see the autoimmune specialist. But I was feeling a lot of physical pain, so I made an appointment with my primary doctor. The pain was so intense I was thinking it might be appendicitis, but my doctor narrowed it down to ovarian pain.

The ultrasound showed a cyst the size of a softball completely covering an ovary. My doctor wasn't even sure if there was an ovary there because the growth was so large. He said if the cyst popped, it would be very painful. If it didn't, it would need to be removed. He prescribed some pain meds, and I waited it out over Thanksgiving. Luckily it popped without much trouble. With this going on amid my dealing with David's death and my marriage crisis, I felt like my body was rejecting me.

I finally got in to see the specialist for autoimmune disease. He briefed me about the specific type of lupus that I had called Sjögren's syndrome. He explained it as a drying disorder that was attacking the mucus membranes in my body. Basically, my body was walling itself up with armor and rigidity. The specialist explained the medications and the list of possible side effects. Medication sounded less than glamorous and seemed to cause more issues than Sjögren's itself. I opted off the medication path and delved into online research on what I could do naturally.

Stress seemed to be the number one culprit of Sjögren's flare-ups, so if I could control my stress, maybe I could manage my symptoms. Controlling my stress was laughable at that point. I knew where the current stress was coming from, but autoimmune diseases don't just pop up overnight. My body had been under stress long before my diagnosis, and I had ignored the signs.

I had this wonderful chiropractor, Liz. She suggested I look deeper into the why of my lupus symptoms and referred me to classical homeopathy. I had never heard of it, but I trusted Liz and decided to make an appointment.

My experience with classical homeopathy made me feel like I was being tossed into the deep end of the pool. My first appointment was two hours of questioning by the practitioner. He was attempting to assess my condition. The goal was to prescribe a natural remedy that spoke to my unique experience. This is my oversimplified explanation of classical homeopathy.

At every session I would try to explain the grief I was feeling over David's passing in an effort to convey my "experience" to my practitioner. My feeling vocabulary at that time was limited to sad, mad, glad. I overgeneralized everything about my experience to make it less distinctive and more like everyone else's. I hadn't realized fitting in wasn't the goal. This behavior wasn't on purpose; it was all I had known. But, for this therapy, my behavior wouldn't work, and I couldn't yet see my way out of the paper bag.

"But how does this experience feel? Explain it to me," my practitioner would repeat.

"You know! How anyone else would feel!" I would say back.

Was he thick? Doesn't he know how death feels? I would think to myself. He didn't want to know how everyone else felt; he was trying desperately for me to explain my experience.

We were not communicating, or I was not understanding. I began to ask myself if he was the crazy one. Why did I have to spell out how I felt about my experience? When you love someone who dies, it's tragic. Everyone experiences it as tragic. Duh! Hadn't he seen Romeo and Juliet?

How did I feel? What did it feel like to me? He wanted me to give examples of what I was experiencing. I was so out of touch with my feelings I didn't know what I was experiencing. I sensed it was grueling for him to try and educate me on my feelings.

I went week after week trying hard to answer his questions the right way. It became a challenge, or a contest, and I couldn't lose. What was he looking for? I went back if only just to master him. I just wanted him to give me the acceptable answer so I could be done.

In the end, I didn't win. I ended up feeling so insecure from not being able to connect to his reasoning that I became defensive and resorted to belittling him. I totally missed the point with classical homeopathic therapy. It produced no results for me because I couldn't — or something in me didn't want to — get in touch with my "experience."

I was looking for a path to healing, or trying to beat down my own weeds to make one. I knew I would eventually begin to see progress. After all, I was seeing some signs, some evidence that there was a solution even if I couldn't be completely honest about my "experience" yet. Opportunities were presenting themselves to me. A whole new world was beginning to open up around me, as if to say, "Look here." I peered in occasionally, like looking into a world of light and clarity, but it felt too bright for me to fully enter. I wasn't sure if I could fake it there, and I knew I wasn't quite ready to get real.

Chapter 5

DIRTY GIRL

One day during an appointment with my obstetrician regarding the cyst, it was noted that my HPV (human papillomavirus) had also flared up, and I needed to schedule for a coloscopy to remove a growth from my cervix. The procedure was scheduled for December 10, the day after my thirty-second birthday.

When I had first met Vince, I was embarrassed to explain to him my sexual history and the details of my sexually transmitted disease. If HPV goes unchecked and untreated, there is a high chance of cervical or ovarian cancer developing, potentially affecting one's ability to have babies. Luckily for me, I didn't want babies, and he didn't want any more. So, that wasn't an issue. The issue was exposing Vince to my HPV. Reportedly, men are rarely affected by any symptoms but can be carriers and transmit it to their female partners, putting their partners at risk.

When I was first diagnosed, my OB told me I had the responsibility to call all the guys I had been sexually active with and report my findings so they could be tested. These were humiliating conversations — with the OB and the few fellows I ashamedly had to tell.

By the time I told Vince about my HPV, I had already called the handful of guys I needed to call. And I do not deny that there were some I chose not to call. One in particular was the one I believed I had contracted the HPV from in the first place. Among the fellows I did call, there was one I didn't treat so well, and I still have remorse over our time together. I won't ever forget the guilt I felt when telling him that he should go get tested. I was sad and ashamed, as if I had betrayed his body, and heart —and I had. Painful. But no one is entirely innocent in reckless sex.

I sat in the doctor's office awaiting the procedure to remove the growth from my cervix. Vince was in the waiting room. I felt teary-eyed and emotional in this sterile room. I recall a conscious choice to push my feelings down . . . aside . . . away. I had to be strong. I couldn't feel pity or embarrassment or risk emotional exposure. I had done this to myself, and I had to face the consequences like a big girl.

I draped the small sheet over my lap and pulled myself into the stirrups. The procedure required long scissors to snip the small growth off the cervix. It would burn a little, and then I would be sore for a few days.

I consciously shifted my thinking to logic and erred on the side of humor.

"Don't snip off too much down there," I said to the doctor. I still need some of that." I laughed.

"We have a comedian here," the doctor said to his nurse.

"I could have probably done this myself at home if you had let me borrow your scissors," I said to distract myself.

I had to laugh so I didn't cry. I didn't want to become emotional. The feeling that I was "dirty" had been triggered.

This whole sexuality thing got off course for me after my divorce from David. I got married just two weeks after I had turned twenty. I had never been sexually active. David was my first boyfriend and the only one I had been with. When we divorced, I became a recluse at my parents' place for a year and saw hardly anyone. It wasn't long, though, before I felt the need for a man, and I found myself on the hunt for human contact.

I always felt a heightened sense of sexuality, and after the divorce, I had embraced it as part of my identity. I was quiet and particular and played a game of wits and conquest. I hadn't realized my need was greater than just human contact and always felt lonely and insatiable.

From a very young age, I was intensely aware of my "dirtiness." Something was bad about my body. I didn't have the vocabulary, knowledge, or emotional intuition to express or categorize how I felt. Since I couldn't make sense of it, I shoved it down and stuffed it out of the way of my day-to-day life.

I just knew I wasn't "right." I was almost afraid of myself, my own sexuality. As I hit puberty, the feelings worsened. I felt guilty for just being. I felt unsafe and uncomfortable in my own skin nearly all the time. I was hypervigilant to make certain I felt, and looked, acceptable so no one would notice my discomfort. I was a great actress — the best.

Sometimes I wondered if part of my feeling dirty came from being molested by a female when I was five, a secret I had kept until my twenties, when I shared it with David. Part of my feeling dirty could have been attributed to family shame: My maternal grandfather had been convicted of sexual abuse in the 1980s. But I had not, until that lunch with Nana, known about Aunt Alpha, so I assumed that couldn't have played a part in my feeling dirty. But even if I had known about Aunt Alpha sooner, would I have connected her experience to my own sense of shame and low self-worth? What else didn't I know?

But here I sat, and at the end of the day, I was my own judge and jury for the things I thought and felt. I deemed myself flawed and dirty — case closed. Wasn't this moment of getting squamous cells from a sexually transmitted disease snipped off my cervix in this sterile doctor's office proof of my incurable filth?

Chapter 6

MISTAKEN IDENTITY

As I continued to read more about what my cells were doing inside my body with my newly diagnosed autoimmune disease, something about misidentification kept popping up. This is my oversimplified version: The white and red blood cells get confused and attack themselves. Mistaken identity. I began to ruminate on where in my life I was experiencing, or had experienced, mistaken identity. Why was I "armoring up"? Had this theme been a part of my story, and was this physical manifestation connected to it?

I have always had a small love affair with words. When I met Vince, I traveled with a pocket thesaurus in my car to read at red lights. I am a notably awful speller and sometimes use the wrong word at the wrong time, but that doesn't change my affection for words. I like to listen to narratives and try to see what may be behind what someone is saying. This love affair is sometimes toxic because digging for a deeper meaning isn't always the best way to walk through life. But sometimes it's helpful, like using a superpower for good and not evil. So when I read over and over that cells attack themselves, I wondered what that meant at a deeper level.

After many days and weeks of reading up on Sjögren's syndrome, I sat back and listened to my own narrative: My cells have mistaken identity. My cells are attacking themselves. I am building armor around myself. I am becoming rigid.

Was my life telling a story through my cells? When I asked myself this question, it resonated with me and reverberated back to my past, and I got chills. I didn't like where this story was going, but I followed it down the rabbit hole a bit more. I needed to tell myself the real story instead of the one I told to look good.

My mother had left my birth father when she was seven months pregnant with me. He had made it clear he did not want to have children and did not want to stay around to be a father to me. Subsequently, a decision was made that she would move in with her boyfriend, and he would become my father. Long story short, I would not know I had two fathers until my parents' tenth wedding anniversary, when they dropped the info bomb during a family camping trip. But just as I had always felt innately dirty, I had also always felt innately out of place in my home as a child, so this news sort of made sense in my core, but not in my mind. Did I know in my soul somehow that my birth father was not in my life?

Speaking the language of my autoimmune disease, I asked the deeper questions: Why was I walling up, becoming rigid, to protect myself? Did I misunderstand myself and misidentify myself? Did I attack myself? Did I hate myself? Did I feel abandoned and ashamed of myself at a core level?

It appeared that my symptoms were saying yes to these questions. But what did that mean for my life? Had I been building my life on a lie? Sjögren's is the drying syndrome, attacking the mucus membranes so that a person hardens and dries up, like an old, crusty riverbed.

I did not like the way I felt, or shall I say, I didn't like the judgment I immediately placed on the way I felt. Self-pity was unattractive to me (although later I learned how much I indulged myself in it). Blame was also unattractive, and so were sorrow and grief. I wasn't going to blame my parents (not yet, anyway). I wasn't going to be sad for myself, and, God forbid, I wasn't going to admit any of this made me sad.

This ball of yarn was all tangled up and in one big, knotted mess. Could I just pull on one string and somehow magically fix it? It seemed it wasn't working out that way. I thought maybe I should just scrap it like some people do every year on Christmas when they realize last year's lights are beyond untangling and so they start fresh with a new box. But this ball, this tangled, mangled mess — it was my soul. The option of tossing it out would be a difficult, but admittedly viable, choice. What else didn't I know?

When I journaled, ugly things came out and showed up on the paper. So I would revert to religion, put my mask back on, and try harder. Couldn't God just fix all of it? Make it easy? A magic potion? I honestly asked myself how long I could live with just some knowledge of my story and pretend the rest was okay — this wadded mess.

I knew there was some trash in the family history, but I could brush that away by making a joke about it. People will laugh at a good redneck joke. I realized my father had left me on what felt like, or seemed like, a simple whim. But lots of people aren't raised by their biological parents, lots of people suffer from autoimmune diseases, and fatigue can easily be excused these days. So my story had nothing to do with this mess. I was just another statistic of the environment.

But if I invalidated my story, I couldn't validate what I was feeling — or didn't feel. I was moving like a robot through life. My memories, what few I had, were garbled and foggy. My second marriage was falling apart. My heart was broken. My days were, at best, blasé. I had no desire to keep living and wondered how life could ever improve. The thoughts of feeling out of place since childhood and being dirty at my core rang in my head and added to the reasons my life felt draining and meaningless.

I wondered how much longer I could go on wearing my masks: tough, funny, and brave. I was the one who said give me a task and I'll dominate it. Give me a person and I'll show them who's boss with brashness; I won't be intimidated. Watch me perform, perfect, and please — and then watch me make it look flawless and authentic. Let me pull you in and let you think I am vulnerable and raw. Let me bring you in just close enough to fool you.

My life was full of people who thought they knew me, but I was alone because they knew only what I wanted them to know. I got good at copying and acting and tweaking the role enough to make it seem like it fit me in true form.

But no one knew me. I didn't even know me. And if I ever stopped just long enough to see the masks I wore, I wanted to vomit. I hated me. I had the diagnosis of mistaken identity, and my cells were attacking me. They didn't know what was good for them because they had got lost in a role and forgot whose side they were on. Confusion abounded. I could save everyone the trouble of finding out I was a fraud and just leave.

But where could I run to and get away from myself? I had two options — keep walking into the story of my life or end it. I couldn't keep living the way things were.

Chapter 7

KIDS

Christmas 2012 came, and I was excited to be finishing the year. Vince and I decided we would take his two daughters to see his family. His parents had just built a new house outside Minneapolis. I don't recall much about this trip except the weather was freezing cold.

We landed in Minneapolis to single-digit temperatures. I had never experienced having a plane deiced at the airport, so that was a first. The plane goes through some chemical spray like a giant car wash. I had also never seen mounds of salt and was confused about why they would have it all over the place. The snow is pretty when it's white but not so pretty when plowed into corners of parking lots to look like mountains of mud. Vince's youngest was eight. She loved the snow and stayed out too long and came in because she couldn't feel her toes anymore.

I felt awkward being around Vince's family and not talking about, or even mentioning, what was happening with our marriage and why he wasn't a touring sound engineer anymore. It was much the same with my family, so I understood the desire to keep the façade going — sweep that dust under the rug (for the time being).

I mechanically moved through the days in the Minneapolis bitter cold, rehearsing deeper ideas in my head but never sharing them. I kept looking toward the future at what I might do next with my life, but the daily tasks seemed to overtake me — or suck me up like a vacuum.

The trip to Minnesota was fairly uneventful, and our next custody hearing with Vince's ex-wife was scheduled for when we got back. Vince had been a touring sound engineer, but since his emotional affair, he had come off the road and was going to college and was making less money. We were hoping for an adjustment in child support and increased visitation with the girls. I was paying the bulk of our bills, while Vince was struggling to pay child support and his daughters' medical coverage, as well as their competitive gymnastics and horseback riding activities, on a reduced income.

Unfortunately, the judge did not grant any changes at the January custody hearing. He wanted to see tax documents showing Vince's actual reduction in income and more proof of longevity, that he would permanently be off the road and at home, before granting increased custody. I was probably hoping for some proof of longevity too.

Much of winter and early spring was spent focusing on both my physical and mental health journey.

Vince was busy, too. In addition to his counseling, he had enrolled in college to find a new vocation and was carrying a full load of classes, and he was also working local shows when he wasn't at school. We did not connect with each other during those months, but I can't say I hated that.

We shared his daughters during spring break, but because Vince's spring break did not coincide with theirs, I took on the responsibility of taking care of them while they were in town. I took them around to visit my friends and my sisters and even took them to work with me when I had no other place for them to go.

I had not yet learned the term co-dependency. I just thought my motivation stemmed from a helpful place, not a controlling one. Maybe if I helped enough and was good enough and supportive enough, I could be loved. So I kept up my old patterns of behavior to earn what I wanted most from Vince, and probably myself, too — love.

The best word to describe those months, or even that year, was vacillation. I vacillated so much between staying the same — buying and selling the story I had come to tell my whole life — and moving in a new direction. Choosing to stay the same meant pressure to keep up the façade. But there were many moments freedom was calling my name, urging me to let down the walls and shake off the chains. A less robotic life. A less programmed life. Maybe a life where I could feel connected, be organic and creative and filled with life. I felt totally bipolar in my pursuits, and I could not seem to commit to one plan or the other.

For the new year I needed something to help my stress levels. I made two decisions: I joined a weekly yoga class at the gym, and I started a group called Night-Caps for Second Wives.

Sometimes, when I look back at those times, I am impressed by certain choices I made (pat on the back, Bethany). The yoga was great for learning breathing exercises and how to stretch and decompress. I ended up really loving it.

The Night-Caps for Second Wives didn't really take off because only one person, Misty, showed up for the meeting. But Misty ended up being a great source of friendship for me during that season. She was a safe person to talk to, with no agenda, and we had a common connection — she was on her second marriage, never had kids, and was a stepmom to a daughter just a few years older than Vince's daughters. She was also a counselor and had a refreshing and positive outlook in my time of need.

I started to see some things from another perspective and began asking myself, How did I find my way into this mess, and how would I find my way out?

Chapter 8

UNBORN

During spring break with Vince's girls, a new issue began to surface — a very personal issue. I began to struggle with my lack of a personal lasting legacy. I imagined Vince in the future with his two girls and grandkids, but I saw me on the outside, or, God forbid, ostracized by them as the "evil stepmom."

I had been putting a lot of energy into Vince's girls, looking after their welfare and best interests. But I was beginning to realize it didn't matter much at the end of the day — they were not my responsibility, and my marriage with Vince at this time was still uncertain. His girls already had a mom, and it wasn't my place to mother them — a fact that was becoming clearer and clearer to me as time passed.

Who was I kidding? I didn't want the responsibility of being a mother. It was an understatement that I didn't want children. Having a baby terrified me. Or did I terrify myself? Either way, the thought of bringing a human being into the world horrified me.

Knowing this, it's surprising how careless I had been with my sex life. I never tried not to get pregnant.

You would think for someone who didn't want a baby, I would have been way more cautious — birth control, double wrapping, all that jazz (I just cracked myself up).

I told myself I couldn't get pregnant. Maybe it was my ovarian issue. Maybe it was my newfound autoimmune disease. But this thought always took second place to another argument — I wasn't destined to have kids. But I did have two pregnancy scares! Was I secretly trying to see if I could get pregnant by being hopelessly reckless with men?

When David and I were married, we actually had the kid conversation a few times, but it always ended the same — our dreams would take priority over starting a family. I am sure David struggled with the reasons behind his choice not to have kids, as did I. After the divorce, I figured I could just marry a man with kids to avoid the entire kiddo topic. That I did. So now why was I revisiting it?

This soul-searching was unearthing new feelings around this issue. It felt somewhat like guilt, mixed with fear and loathing. Did I have the power to intentionally mess with destiny by avoiding a baby? Whispers of an unborn child began to haunt me, saying, "I am supposed to be here, but you are too selfish to even consider having me." Talk about creepy.

These whispers kept me up at night and caused me to feel anguish and despair over my future. After about a month of this restlessness, I decided to write about these feelings. It was a warm evening, and I was home alone. I went over to the convenience store and picked up a cigar and a can of pre-mixed malt liquor (this is not a joke). I sat on my front porch and cracked open my journal. It wasn't long before my defenses fell. Cheap cigars and booze will do that rather quickly.

My scribbles summarized my reasons for not having a child. Sadly, the truth showed how I wished I wasn't alive. I free wrote about the mistake of my own conception — my mom's unplanned pregnancy with me and my biological father stepping out of my life before I ever knew him, and then their separation and divorce. I had deep-seated feelings of abandonment and not being wanted. I wrote how I felt my existence was an accident and how I was inherently bad and dirty. The last thought echoed my recent journey, and I began to see the dots connecting to something internally significant.

As I sat in the dark on the patio, buzzed, my mind replayed a conversation from years before during a pregnancy scare with a guy I had dated.

"Thank goodness!" he said when I told him I wasn't pregnant. He paused and then continued with this brash statement: "Not that you would make a bad mother. I am just relieved you're not pregnant."

The pause and the statement "Not that you would make a bad mother" filled me with alarm, since I didn't think I would have made a good mother. And I started to wonder if maybe my destiny was set, or was I supposed to choose?

I was spinning and slipping in and out of depression thinking about it too much. The pain of these thoughts stirred up the desire to escape my own skin, run away from my own thought process. What in the world was I unearthing?

I settled it by asking Vince to schedule a vasectomy consultation.

"This will be like Russian roulette. You have a limited window of time to pull the trigger and land a bullet," I joked halfheartedly to God (or maybe it was a prayer).

I called my mentor, Cathy, several times over the next weeks and months. I was spinning out with worry and struggled to reconcile with what destiny might have planned for me. Was my life already predestined, or was there actually free will? What if we all actually had free will? How was I supposed to know what was good for me? I had no sense of self-trust. I was beginning to see how clueless I was about the deeper things of life.

Chapter 9

MORE LOSS

The one-year anniversary of David's death was approaching, and I couldn't believe so much time had passed. Processing my grief over his death, as well as the betrayal in my marriage, the heavy questions about my family, and my autoimmune disease was all-consuming. I was still managing to work my day job, although I'm not sure how well I was producing. I had stopped spending time with friends, and I tried to steer clear of my family. I didn't know how to be. I felt the reality of my inauthentic self and couldn't bear the tension of the incongruency.

The morning of May 25, 2013, I was getting ready for Sunday morning church when my phone rang. It was my pastor, Tracy. She asked if Vince was home with me — it felt like bad news. I told her that he was, so she proceeded.

"Racquel died last night in a car wreck on her way home from work," she said.

I didn't know what to say.

Racquel was a high school friend who had attended church with David and me. She played guitar in a band with David. Racquel and her mom played

"Communion Song" during my wedding. I had been bracing myself for the one-year anniversary of David's passing but not for a new shock. I began to feel like I was in the movie Final Destination and worried who would go next.

My pastor suggested I wait for David's mom outside church to tell her the news.

"Yes, of course I will," I answered.

As I waited outside church with Vince, a few other people lingered steps away. I could see the worry in their eyes for what I might be feeling, what would happen when Tina arrived, and how I would handle the task. Tina arrived with her husband, and as they walked up to me, I asked Tina to sit down on a bench.

How does one do this? I didn't know. I was making it up as I went. I put my hands on hers. Just like I had known when my pastor called me, Tina knew I had bad news.

"Racquel passed away last night in an auto wreck." I came right out with it.

Tears rolled down her face as she gazed into the distance. Sadness rolled in around us like dark storm clouds. Her husband stood at a distance in silence.

The people who had been standing around the periphery seemed to be slowly closing in, as if they felt a responsibility to offer condolences. Tina began to feel suffocated and said she had to leave, she couldn't be there. I felt helpless. I walked her back to the car she had just emerged from, and her husband drove her home.

Racquel's death produced a few tears and a few days of sorrow. I had been reckoning David's death in deep ways for almost a year. I had been reckoning my family's dysfunction and my illness. I was vibrating at deep levels. I wondered if I was callous to her death somehow. I figured I should have felt more grief.

The following week Vince was working the annual Ojai Jazz Festival like he had the year before. We stayed in the same hotel where we were the night Tina had called about David's passing. Just shy of one year since David's funeral, I drove from the hotel in Ojai to Racquel's funeral. Once again, family and friends, who had gathered the year before, all crammed into another church to grieve another young life gone too soon.

Racquel was an only child. She had been married only a few years and was considering starting a family. As I visited her mother over the following weeks, I was overwhelmed with the thought of her missing legacy. Racquel's mom and dad had divorced when she was a baby; her mother tenaciously raised Racquel without help. Her life was essentially all things Racquel — so much so that she had remained single to focus on her daughter. Now, it was just her. These facts were heavy and caused me to think that even if I decided to have a child, I couldn't depend on that child to be my legacy.

Racquel's passing. The Russian roulette. Not trusting myself — all these factors added up to one sure thing: Vince and I would schedule a consultation for him to get snipped.

Nothing in life is guaranteed.

Chapter 10

CONTROL

Nothing is guaranteed, but maybe I could arrange my outcomes better. I began to ponder what other legacy I could leave if I decided not to have children. I felt uneasy in my skin; I needed a path that was more within my control. With Racquel's passing atop David's passing, I was perplexed by the concept of death. I added it to the "con" side of the pros and cons regarding having children and saw it as a reason to focus on things I could control. I sensed my desire to control was unhealthy, but I needed to grab on to something and manipulate it into an outcome that felt satisfying.

I went on a control rampage. I knew how to "perform and perfect." Even if my former ways hadn't worked and made me sick, I needed do to something to control my outcomes and take the focus off the darkness in my life.

I knew what I could do! I would apply for Dr. Henry Cloud and Dr. John Townsend's year-long Life Coach Experience, which was a program to help professionals set and reach their career goals. I had applied before but wasn't accepted. But maybe this would be my year. Maybe this could be the thing that could calm my turmoil.

I got to work on the application for the Life Coach Experience. I had to choose a serious goal and show I had the necessary experience in my profession to be considered for the program. I had a lot of goals to choose from, but my main goal would be acceptance into a graduate program. I structured my application for the Life Coach Experience to show my good side and dull the darkness of my inner storm.

I was so optimistic about getting into the Life Coach Experience, and subsequently getting into a graduate program, that I reviewed all my old coursework, talked to some former psychology professors, and decided I would need to do some prep work. It was fairly unanimous that I would need a statistics-level math course for graduate study research.

I hate math. I suck at math, and I had hoped to never step foot into another math class again. I literally had to take my upper division math classes three times each to earn my undergrad degree, which was in sociology and communications. Even then, my diploma was delayed because I had failed my last math class. Did I mention, I hate math! But it was a great distraction, so I bit the bullet and signed up for a summer statistics course.

I was also accepted into the Life Coach Experience. It felt good to be moving toward goals that didn't feel as burdensome as the grief I was wading through. Back to the rational, away from the emotional. I had things to manipulate into satisfying outcomes.

If controlling my situation and proving myself was possible, I did it in my statistics class. After our first big test, the professor projected the class grades onto an overhead screen. We were in a fairly large lecture hall with stadium seating. The class was full, and I was curious how I would rank. Holy cow, Batman! I scored highest in the class! What the hell?

I took the class very seriously, as if my future depended on it (it didn't). Who would have known that statistics could be such a great diversion from life? I could perform, perfect, and please all in one place. Did I mention I wanted to sit in the front row and bring cookies to the professor? Vince advised against it.

Proving myself in the Life Coach Experience was harder to do than in my math class — and turned out to be embarrassing. Dr. Cloud was traveling at the start of the course, so Dr. Townsend facilitated our first two months with no sight of Dr. Cloud. I liked Dr. Townsend, but I really enjoyed Dr. Cloud's work. In August, when Dr. Cloud did show up, I decided to be a smartass about him not showing up until then.

We were all sitting around tables in our smaller cohort groups waiting for Dr. Townsend to begin when I saw Dr. Cloud walk through the back door. I got giddy on the inside. But God forbid I show the childish emotions of joy and excitement! Instead, I used good old humor to deflect my vulnerable giddiness and made a memorable moment of it — embarrassingly memorable.

"It's nice of you to finally grace us with your presence!" I snarked smartly, half under my breath. Except Dr. Cloud heard me loud and clear. I was hoping only the people in my group would hear me and laugh. I would gain popularity as the funny girl.

First of all, who in the world did I think I was? I had not even been properly introduced to Dr. Cloud yet. He knew nothing of my admiration for his work, let alone my "smartassisms." I actually wanted nothing more than to be accepted and welcomed by him. Instead, I was the little girl on the playground trying to get attention by throwing rocks.

As Dr. Cloud passed my table, he stopped, looked down at me, and paused to think about how to reply to my comment.

"Father issues? No, it's mother issues," he said with a discerning smirk and continued to the front to start the class.

My friend sitting next to me held back laughter with tight lips and big eyes, watching me as my expression changed from smartass to wounded. It was so awful. It was too accurate not to be painful.

Managing outcomes would remain my hideout for a while. I surmised grazing the surface of my darkness was too uncomfortable. I had done enough digging to satisfy my curiosity for the time being. I had done enough emotional work to use the excuse, "I've already tried that."

Chapter 11

HYPONOTHERAPY

That summer, as if it were meant to be, a hypnotherapist rented space in the office next door to mine. I did not have a good opinion of hypnotherapy at the time and thought it was a form of spiritualism. I was leery of it. It was just too weird for me. I already had enough junk to muddle through without adding to it, but this therapist strangely piqued my interest.

I bumped into him in the parking lot, and he struck up a conversation with me. He told me he was a Christian. I thought that was weird. I had never heard of Christian hypnotherapy. That evening I chatted with Vince about making an appointment to try it under the guise of "biblical" direction. We agreed, and I made an appointment.

At my appointment, I looked around for the long gold chain and pocket watch that he would be swinging in front of my eyes. No gold watch to be found. The therapist explained to me that he would use words to guide the session. I would close my eyes, listen, and watch with my mind's eye. I laughed out loud at him. I would watch with my mind's eye? I wanted to reply in some sarcastic way to imply I thought this was superstitious, but I refrained. Instead, I paused awkwardly, shrugged, and sheepishly sank back into my chair.

Delving into the darkness in my life, we talked about all I was struggling with. He was another proponent of the idea that I held a greater connection with Aunt Alpha than just our bloodline. Just what that was, was for me to find out.

He explained he would guide me into my own subconscious by walking me into a sacred space with words and see what I would learn.

"Close your eyes and walk, in your mind's eye, to a place where you feel comfortable." He paused and then continued. "Where are you? Where did you arrive?"

"I am beside a Jacuzzi in a tropical-forest-looking place, near a translucent ocean and white sand," I answered.

"Get into the Jacuzzi and begin to walk down into it," he said.

So I did. I walked down a spiral staircase deeper and deeper into the Jacuzzi. I was in an underwater world much larger than it appeared from the outside.

It was peaceful, serene. I won't ever forget the feeling. Yet I didn't know what I was doing there or where I was. I couldn't see much or understand much about this place. I looked around for what seemed like one or two minutes before I heard his next command.

"Begin to walk up the staircase and out of the Jacuzzi," he directed.

I emerged from the Jacuzzi, and, still in my mind's eye, he was there to walk me back down the beach to the office and the chair in which I was sitting. Then he asked me to open my eyes. That was it? He said it had been twenty minutes! It was so strange.

Had I continued to do more work with him maybe eventually I could have learned something from my subconscious about my darkness. But he ended up leaving that location a few months after he began renting there, and that was my only session. However, that one experience invited me to look deeper, but it would be a long time before I connected again to that place in my subconscious.

Chapter 12

THE SNIP

The following week, Vince and I went to his vasectomy consultation, which felt more like "Spouse Approval Day." You would think with the term consultation, you would be consulting the doctor. But what really happens is that the doctor consults the wife for her approval. "Tell your wife to come in so we can drill down on how this process is mostly permanent and she can sign a 'I said it's okay' form." I am not sure if all doctors' offices do this, or if it was because I had no kids of my own, or if it was just this office's policy to make sure the wife was on board before the husband shut down his seed factory.

Although my feelings were completely convoluted on the whole thing, I assured our doctor that I didn't have any hesitation. I wanted to say, "Hey, Doc, I've never been pregnant, probably can't get pregnant, am terrified to have a baby, and don't want to play anymore, so snip the boy — and do it fast!" We got the official nod, signed the forms, and scheduled the vasectomy for September.

Between the time of Vince's consultation and his procedure, I was looking for a naturopathic doctor to treat my lupus. Although I didn't care for needles, our friends swore by an acupuncturist in San Diego. It turned out autoimmunity was her specialty. I had my first session with her in mid-August and felt wonderful, better than any other treatment I'd tried to this point.

I liked her right away. She explained how Eastern medicine had more natural ways to assist my body with my drying disorder. Her goal was to get me fluid and unstuck.

Oh boy, did I feel fluid! She must have stuck me with a love potion, too, because I was super frisky. Unfortunately for me, Vince had to work that night, but the love potion was so strong I waited up well past midnight for him to get home. He was tired, but I didn't care — the die had been cast. You know what I'm talkin' about.

As the summer of 2013 came to an end, so did my statistics class. Grades were posted — I passed with an A! I could not believe it, I was so happy. Vince thought we should celebrate. He planned a car-camping road trip in his 1978 Volkswagen over Labor Day weekend. I saw us as two vagabonds searching for our way back to love and had glimpses of happy moments. I soaked up the sun that peeked through the proverbial dark clouds and hoped new weather was coming.

Shortly after we arrived back from our road trip, I had my third pregnancy scare. The other two had been during my single years, but I never had a positive pregnancy test. This time I was married and just as worried.

My chiropractor, Liz, wanted me to show her a house that was for sale, and after the showing I told her I would be picking up a pregnancy test at the pharmacy. She was beaming with happiness. Her face was a face I wouldn't forget.

I shot back a pinched expression.

"You think that's funny, don't you?" I snarked.

She knew about my hesitation around the topic of pregnancy, and although she didn't pressure me in any particular direction, I knew she hoped I would experience having a child of my own.

I stopped by the pharmacy on my way back to the office and took the test in the office bathroom, following the directions just like the times before. But this time I watched as a soft pink line began to emerge. The test was positive. Shit! What? How in the world?

What would I do? I figured Vince needed to know, so I called and asked if he would go on lunch break with me. Then I texted him a photo of the pregnancy test. I don't honestly recall his response. But he agreed to take a break from work so we could stare in silence together. I picked him up and we drove into a local neighborhood, parked under a big pine tree, and sat in silence for a long time before we both shrugged. It was the love potion!

"Should I still get the vasectomy?" he asked.

"Of course. There is no guarantee this will stick," I replied emphatically.

I was in shock. I was hoping it would all just blow over and my period would come just like it did the other times. But this time I actually had a positive pregnancy test. This time I could not tell myself that this was only a scare.

Chapter 13

LEGACY OF BROKENNESS

The positive pregnancy test launched me into acute self-awareness. I knew I was in some denial about my family of origin and how its darkness was impacting me. I would feel my badness and then detach from my story. It was months since I had begun to look specifically at my family and the struggles they faced as the source of my dark feelings, but I had turned away from all that information and swung back to rational control.

But if I was pregnant, and I was, I would have to get serious about my life and my healing. I would have to. As I circled around again to my family, this time I would need to go a little deeper into the dark.

I started where I left off. The story I had always told myself. My parents were married. I grew up in church. We always had food. I was never homeless. I was a middle child with two healthy sisters. We were a homeschool family. I was a solid rule-follower with good grades. We had no major issues. I could tell myself this story, "my story," over and over. I had told it to other people over the years to reinforce it and had received kudos for such a wonderful story, which made me want to do even more good things, overachieving things.

"Yep. Sounds good. Well-painted picture," I would tell myself.

So, what was the problem? Why were my feelings and my body telling another story? None of "my story" was a lie. It just wasn't the whole truth. This other story, the one my feelings and body were telling me, was beckoning me to go deeper into the truth, and I was beginning to realize what I would find there was the darkness.

When you are used to the dark, sometimes the light is painful. So I would avoid looking at the truth by concluding over and over again that the problem must be in my head. The problem was me. I was inherently broken inside for some reason I didn't know. Why did I have to try so hard to behave like people around me, or behave better? I strived to succeed beyond the average person in order to prove nothing was wrong with me. If only somehow I could prove it to myself.

I could blame my feeling different on being homeschooled or being brought up in a religious home, but I reminded myself of the Wizard of Oz. He had worked pretty darn hard to cover his insecurities: "Look over there! Don't look behind the curtain!"

But even though I told myself the story I had always told over and over, I couldn't honestly connect to it. It was just a story, and either it was an untrue one or something was missing because "my story" didn't resonate with me. Sometimes I sensed I told myself the story over and over to protect something I innately knew but was subconsciously covering up. Was this "something" beginning to emerge from under the surface, unable to hide anymore and triggered by the pain of my relationships with David and Vince?

I was the "roadie wife." I was a divorcée. I was hopelessly reckless between marriages. I was searching for something. But for what? And why? These identities of mine were so disconnected from the overarching story I had crafted.

I had been sheltered — homeschooled from second grade until college. I grew up religious — the good girl who never dated until I was seventeen. I was proud of the fact that David was the first boy I had ever kissed or dated. I didn't lie (knowingly), cuss or drink. I respected my elders and had a job since I was fifteen years old. My dad taught me the value of hard work and money, and my mom taught me the importance of faith. Everything looked right. Then what happened? One day I snapped, and my body turned against me? I don't think so. Something was going on behind the scenes I hadn't noticed.

It was true. From the outside everything looked good. And my parents were still together, which was important for my mom to note on occasion. She took a lot of pride in that just like I took pride in my purity with David.

But none of this was the actual truth. My real parents were not together, even if that is what we told people. Very few knew my dad wasn't my biological father, that my biological father had left me before I was born.

My behavior toward the end of my marriage with David, and thereafter, was completely irresponsible and incongruent with the picture I had painted of myself. It was showing a shadow of the darkness below the surface. My symptoms were telling me, "You can't live apart from your true story" (as someone I respect always says).

What was happening below the surface? I had to look at some obvious truths. Like, even if my parents were together, they were not happy. I witnessed years of uneasiness between them. They were never openly loving or affectionate. Worse, there were some very dark years when their fighting held my sisters and me prisoners in our rooms. More than once I would cry while listening to them shout at each other as I wondered whether either of them would still be around the next day.

My plan to survive what was going on had a deep and toxic religious undertone to it. I would replay my plan every time I heard my parents shouting: I will have to stay with my dad because he will need someone with faith to help him see the light. My father was a professed atheist when we were young. What ten-year-old would need to have that conversation with herself if all was well emotionally in the home?

It was clear to us that Dad had slipped into a depression when the market crashed in the late '80s and he lost his job. Life in California was not going the way he had anticipated when he moved us from Kansas. (The Wizard of Oz reference feels more apropos now.) As a child, I had to be careful and quiet. Don't be a greater burden. Don't make Dad upset. It was critical that I do everything to keep Dad around.

When the market crashed, we moved from a decent townhome to a tiny two-bedroom apartment in the ghetto. Dad was drinking a lot and taking us to some unsavory parties when my mom was working nights. My sisters and I sat white-knuckled in the back seat of the car when he would drink and drive. Mom was livid when she found out. The drinking and the parties were typically the topic of their shouting.

It was during this season of my parents' marital uncertainty that they informed us kids, during a camping trip, that my older sister and I were not our dad's biological children. That moment will always be etched into my brain as one of the worse moments in my history. Deep heartbreak accompanied a strange yet familiar feeling of fear and uncertainty — I wasn't wanted, and I wasn't loved. I ran away from the campfire into my tent, zipped it closed, and bawled alone for what felt like hours. I have a vague memory of one of my parents trying to console me for a brief period from outside my tent but gave up when they realized I was inconsolable.

After the camping trip, we never spoke about my adoption, my birth father, or even the camping trip itself except for a few awkward moments when, for reasons unknown to me, my mom would bring it up.

Then there was my religious upbringing — it was good and bad. In the '80s and '90s, it seemed like a legitimate story: Good girls go to church. Now, looking back, I see it more clearly. Church was a club people attended for a handful of reasons. Some were legitimate Jesus followers. Others were blatantly wounded and hoping that religion would fix them. And the rest seemed to be judgmental, ridged people who were critical perfectionists keeping up a façade. I know I bounced between all three groups for many years trying to earn my salvation, trying to feel less dirty, worthy enough for Jesus to cure me.

I was discovering my sense of darkness didn't start with me. My mom and dad and birth father all had similar, more daunting stories of trauma, abuse, and disconnect in their upbringing. As I peeked further back into my family's history, I lifted more and more veils in order to see the real human condition of trauma and undealt-with toxic family patterns. The reality of my family's disconnect from the truth was clearly becoming the epicenter of my own disconnect as an adult.

As I pressed into finding more pieces of my puzzle, I decided I would follow the rabbit and went headlong into interviewing aunts, grandparents, and my parents about our family story. Each person held a piece of the puzzle, their story as seen through their own eyes, and as I listened to their stories, the picture as a whole came into focus. One thing was for sure — I began to feel uneasy about bringing a baby into the world, or shall I say, into my legacy of brokenness.

Chapter 14

PREGNANCY

Vince and I were stumped about how to handle the pregnancy. I didn't know what to do. The idea of having a baby being a matter of fate or free will didn't seem to matter now, and I didn't like that it was out of my control. But since I am a fairly responsible person, I knew I needed to look for an OB and make an appointment.

However, I was just getting used to the idea of moving back into a more comfortable environment of having some control with my Life Coach Experience and finding a graduate program to attend. What would this wrench do to my plans? I decided to wait a few weeks and Google next steps on the internet before deciding to see an OB.

Since Vince had left his job as a touring engineer during our marriage crisis and was no longer on the road, he worked local gigs while he attended college. But "local" meant the southern territory from Los Angeles across to Las Vegas and down to San Diego. He for sure was not getting attached to the pregnancy idea. I guess, for the time being anyway, it changed his life less than it changed mine (except for my occasional flatulence that he had to endure).

Sometimes his local gigs were cool, and I would tag along so we could spend time together. Just after I found out we were pregnant, he was assigned an event that sounded interesting in the Topanga hills above Malibu Beach. I had been to Malibu the previous year, when I stole a beer mug from the Malibu Inn. This time it would be different, though — no tour buses, no awkward walk-ins on tour managers and unsavory women. This was a fundraiser for veterans, first responders, and trauma survivors, and Rick Allen, the drummer for the band Def Leppard, was hosting the event. That sounded pretty epic to me. I couldn't pick Def Leppard out in a crowd or identify their music, but I knew the name and that they were fairly famous.

Upon arriving at the old red brick Topanga Community Center, I realized this fundraiser was also a drum circle. I found Vince, who brought me up to speed on the whole event. I learned that Rick Allen had only one arm (me — cheesy, ignorant Classic Rock smile). I had no idea. Don't drummers need two hands to properly do their job? I hadn't known that he had lost his arm in an accident in the '80s, and in a little less than two years was back playing for the band — and plays in the band to date. I was impressed with this type of resilience.

Vince also dropped another piece of information on me that was much more personal — I had to drum. I had to what? I wasn't trying to be rude, but I hadn't gone there to drum. I went to hang around the sidelines. I wanted to turn and leave.

I didn't even have a drum! No drum? We've got you covered! The sponsors brought out tons of spare drums for people who needed one. Apparently, I needed one. This was so incredibly difficult for me. I felt so awkward and out of place, but it was either run away or drum.

So, in the spirit of silent worship, I cuddled up around my drum on the floor and shut my eyes awaiting next instructions. It was simple. We would bang on the drums together and play along with Rick until everyone was tired and hot. And that's what we did. I played drums with Def Leppard that night. That happened.

Eight weeks into my pregnancy, I found an OB, Dr. Damon Cobb. Vince had an instant man crush on him, (and if you ever met Dr. Cobb, you would know why). He confirmed that I was indeed pregnant and gave Vince and me the simple rundown on what to expect while I was expecting and when to come see him again. I informed him that I wanted the least intrusive pregnancy plan and the fewest appointments possible, as I didn't want to be in his office or be probed more than absolutely necessary.

I anticipated a miscarriage every day while waiting for the first trimester to pass. Dr. Cobb had mentioned that most miscarriages happen in the first trimester, and then I would be over the risk hump. So we waited. Vince didn't want to even admit I was pregnant.

I think he was fairly sure I would miscarry and did not want to be connected to a pregnancy in any way.

Sure enough, around twelve weeks I was still pregnant, and we decided to tell the family. But Vince would still wait for the baby to arrive before getting attached. I was sure we were having a boy. I was mostly sure of this because I didn't want to have a girl. I worked on boy names until I came up with the perfect one, which had a beautiful meaning for me — Levi Giuseppe.

We had our appointment to confirm the sex of the baby. I was hopeful. Then it happened. Dr. Cobb confirmed our baby would be a girl. My heart sank.

I was so angry. I was angry at God. How could He! Why would He? I came home from the appointment and crumbled into the couch in agony. In that moment, I sank under waves of anguish and heartbreak. Furious with God, enraged that I was pregnant, indignant that I was having a girl, I wailed and wailed and wanted to run far, far away from everything — from me, from the world, from Vince, and from the pregnancy. I wanted to run from the future I didn't want for myself. I must have been crying for nearly an hour when I suddenly stopped, almost in a panic that the baby could sense my sorrow.

With that sudden stop, I realized my fear. My sorrow was coming down to me from past generations, and from my own pain. The darkness was beckoning to me. I couldn't bring a girl into this world to be traumatized and victimized like I had been, like the women in my family had been. I thought that if I had a boy, I could somehow save myself the pain of seeing another generation ruined.

I was crying because it seemed everything was all out of my control. But when I stopped crying and acknowledged my fear, I also had a flash of understanding. Some things were very much in my control. One of them was how I could raise this little baby girl. I could do things differently. I could choose — right now — to do things differently. I could embrace this as my opportunity. I could want this. I would never cause this baby girl to feel unwanted, unloved, or unprotected as long as she depended on me.

In that moment I resolved to want this baby inside me, to want her to be a girl, to want to raise her to feel and understand her value and worth. It was a wave of supernatural light that I was grateful to see. God heard me on the couch, and He wanted me to hear Him. I heard Him clearly, and right then and there, I wouldn't have Levi, I would have Livvy Lou.

Chapter 15

BEST BIRTH

Pregnancy was the beginning of something new. I wholeheartedly decided that, if it depended on me, I would exude to Livvy the feeling that she was wanted and loved. But the thought of giving birth to a human being that would literally come out of my body was another thought altogether. Have you ever really thought about this? It's quite repulsive and miraculous and sci-fi and strange. A body comes out of another body!

YouTube birth videos slowly became my obsession. I watched videos on everything from contractions to this stuff called the afterbirth. Wow! Ignorance is bliss.

I needed more. Since I love books, I found a bunch at the library. I wanted to make plans. Shocker, right? Me and plans. Sounded like a plan. I browsed the library looking for books on pregnancy, birth, and what to expect and came across some on pregnancy, birth, and the connection to sexual trauma! I slid a few of those into my basket.

I knew the idea of breastfeeding sketched me out. Was this related to my darkness? I had to know more. I knew that we mammals were created to breastfeed, so it would be the most natural thing for the baby. I read that breast milk was the healthiest milk for the baby (I guess God has some good ideas) and that breastfeeding fostered other baby/mama benefits including bonding with the baby. Since I was afraid that Livvy would not bond with me, I planned to breastfeed even if it creeped me out.

I wasn't sure what bonding meant, or how it would look. I had so many questions. Most of the questions no one could really answer for me. It would be a wait-and-see situation.

I read the book Your Best Birth: Know All Your Options, Discover the Natural Choices, and Take Back the Birth Experience by Ricki Lake. The chapter on sexual trauma, birth dissociation, and fear created a visceral response inside me. It wasn't an accident that I was terrified of birthing, breastfeeding, and bringing up a baby. Studies show that many women shut down emotionally while giving birth or have trauma triggers because of past sexual trauma. Some women may subconsciously shut down contractions or even fail to allow their bodies to produce breast milk due to their fear. This was illuminating to me. The book didn't connect to family trauma, but I wondered if there was a link. Was this my connection to Aunt Alpha? To others in my family with their own stories? I sensed it was.

If the body keeps score of past sexual trauma, and the sex organs and reproductive organs are so intimately related, it was becoming clear to me how this affected women's decisions on giving birth and breastfeeding. I was making mental notes.

I reached forty weeks and was still working full time, but my boss sent me home to start maternity leave. He was afraid my water would break on the office carpet. This pregnancy was replacing my graduate program ambition. But I continued my Life Coach Experience, pregnant and all. Let's just say I "grew" more that year than anyone in the class (wink). But without work, I was left just hanging around the house, which meant I was stuck with me and my mind. I didn't like that, so I tried to stay occupied. I drafted plans about returning to work after having Livvy and how I could get back to my graduate program goals. I sketched drawings and doodled and rented some funny movies from the library. I waited and waited.

While I waited, I learned that most doctors and midwives won't allow a pregnancy to continue past forty-two weeks without inducing labor. Although Dr. Cobb was on the natural side of things, he was no different on this matter. Time was ticking toward an induction date, but I badly wanted Livvy to come on her own time and naturally, since that's what I had read would be best. I thought that if I could change my fear about the delivery, maybe she would happily arrive on time. But no matter how much I tried, I couldn't really grapple with the reality of it. I really hoped she would cooperate before the deadline.

At forty-one weeks and six days, my acupuncturist recommended I visit her friend, Dr. Stan, who helped women go into labor. I took her advice.

After all, she got me into this with her "love potion," I guessed she would get Livvy out. Dr. Stan was concerned that Livvy may have been sunny side up. He did some hands-on maneuvering with my belly, and then Vince and I headed out for a walk. Within an hour my contractions began.

"It's time to head home," I said.

"It worked?" Vince asked.

"I think so. I don't think these are fake contractions since I am almost forty-two weeks along," I nervously replied.

Chapter 16

LIVVY LOU

We headed home and I sat down in the May sunshine and drew a picture with colored pencils. It was a welcome picture that read, "Come out and play, Livvy Lou." The contractions lasted through dinner and into bedtime. I woke to pain I couldn't sleep through. Vince called our doula, who headed over to our house. It felt like the night went on and on. We did a great amount of laboring at home on a yoga ball and breathing and resting until the contractions were close enough the doula recommended we head to the hospital.

Riding in the car, I squinted and squirmed.

"This whole car riding thing with contractions is a dumb idea," I said during a contraction break.

The pain was too much for me to sit still when the wave came.

"Sorry," Vince said, trying to drive safely as he waited for the next contraction to come.

The moments seemed to have all blurred together. We had done a Pre-Check at our hospital, so it was fairly easy to get my room. Vince taped a sign on the door: "No visitors." He told the nurses and doctors not to come in unless necessary. He turned on our battery-operated candles and some peaceful birthing music and ran me a bath.

Vince was doing all he could to create a peaceful environment for me to bring Livvy into the world, and Dr. Cobb was so accommodating and made sure our wishes were respected.

The labor pains continued as the sunrise crept through my hospital window. Despite the intensity, I wasn't dilating. I bathed. I showered. Vince rubbed my back. I was in and out of awareness as our doula coached me on breathing. When I forgot to breathe deeply, she would gently breathe along with me, reminding me to stay in rhythm. Hours passed, and I had moved to only one or two centimeters. We were nearing dinnertime again, and still my water had not broken.

Dr. Cobb informed me that we were at the forty-two-week mark, but since I was laboring heavily, he would let me go without Pitocin to induce. He finished by softy telling me that my energy levels were diminishing. He was concerned I wouldn't have enough to push through to delivery once dilated.

I walked the room in agony.

"I am going to vomit, the pain is so bad," I said.

Vince grabbed the trash can as I leaned over to vomit. I was crying and laughing as I started to pee myself because of the pressure between the vomiting and the contraction.

"Grab a towel!" I laughed and cried.

"I can't hold the trash can and grab a towel," Vince said.

Our doula came to the rescue. And the next three times the contractions came, the same thing happened. I was getting weaker.

Vince drew another bath for my back pain, and I slid in.

"I want to go home now. I am done with this. I can't do this." I cried in fear and exhaustion.

"You can. You will," Vince said softly.

Our doula came over, and Vince stepped away. It was the first time he left my side since my adjustment with Dr. Stan. I sat there in between contractions, in what felt like a time warp, and cried. I had been in labor for twenty-four hours. I whispered to God for help.

"What do I do? I need You, God. I trust You," I said.

I heard the faintest reply, one I will never forget for the rest of my life: "I trust you, Bethany. You can make a good choice."

I sat in silence. I cried. Then I decided for myself. For Livvy. I asked the doula to get Vince.

Vince came back and queried me just to make sure I was sure. An epidural hadn't been part of our plan, but he went to tell the nurse I wanted one. When the anesthesiologist came to administer the spinal tap, I was scared. Vince sat across from me. Husbands aren't allowed to stand anymore because, I guess, guys pass out during this part and cause more issues for the nurses. Tears rolled down my face. Was I making the right choice for Livvy?

With the drugs in me, I now had to lie down. It wasn't long before I realized the pain medication didn't take on the left and I could still feel the back labor. However, I had enough relief for small naps between my big contractions. My rest was twofold because it also relieved Vince and our doula to eat for the first time. They ordered Thai food. The delivery man brought their food to our hospital door. They ate and decompressed while I went in and out of sleep.

During one of my contractions, an on-call doctor came to check my dilation.

"I am not happy with your progress. I recommend breaking your water," she said.

"We will think about it," I replied.

Vince and I chatted with our doula. What were the pros and cons? It really didn't seem like Livvy wanted out, and the sun was setting on a forty-two-week gestation. With much hesitation, I agreed it may help me dilate. So the doctor went ahead and broke my water, and again we waited. With the contractions staying consistent and my body not dilating, the next best bet would be Pitocin. So, I asked for Dr. Cobb.

"We can give you just a little Pitocin and see if it helps to get you going. We need your energy up to get through the pushing. Otherwise, I am worried you will end up with an emergency caesarean," Dr. Cobb advised.

"Okay, I will do it." I reluctantly agreed to try a little.

Then, as the contractions seemed to ramp up with the drugs, the hours continued on, and my body was slowly dilating. Finally, around midnight, I entered the pushing stage. She would finally make her arrival! But the pushing continued for hours and hours. Another day was dawning, and Dr. Cobb let us know she was trying to come, but she was getting stuck sideways. He felt like he could use the vacuum to suction her out. This could be the last resort before caesarean.

We gave the thumbs-up. With that, a whole team of nurses came flooding into the room. It was game on. Livvy needed to come out now. Dr. Cobb then realized the umbilical cord was wrapped around her neck. Not once. Not twice. But three times. She couldn't get out. It would be a three-second ride between unwrapping and vacuum. He worked quick, and I pushed when he gave the order. Within moments Livvy rushed out and swam up on my chest with eyes wide open looking directly at me. She cried for a short moment until Vince came close and whispered to her, "It's Daddy, Livvy. You are here now. It's Daddy. You're safe."

She cuddled up to me, chest on chest, and began breastfeeding without invitation or instruction. She was home, right where she needed to be.

Minutes later, while I was rubbing her vernix into her skin, she pooped all over me. I was so naïve I thought somehow it was melted chocolate.

"How in the world did I get melted chocolate on me?" I said out loud.

"It's meconium, not chocolate," our doula said with a laugh.

Livvy had a bruise on her eyebrow from hitting my pelvic bone over and over while trying to exit. She was indeed our Peaceful Warrior.

Livvy Lou Luchetta arrived 5:26 a.m., May 23, 2014: 8 lbs. 2 oz. and 20 inches.

The next day Livvy lay in the baby incubator next to me. She was born with jaundice and needed to stay until they cleared her. Vince and I were both relieved and blessed. It was then, while resting and watching Livvy sleep, that he told me why he had slipped away when I was crying in the bath during my labor. He was scared and felt so helpless. He could not rescue me, and there was nothing more he could do to get Livvy out safely and quickly. In the moments I was crying and praying to God for answers, he was in the hallway crying and doing the same. Those were the moments when I had made the decision for the epidural and to trust my instinct to rest before needing to push.

Chapter 17

WORK

My mom and dad had moved to Hawaii back in 2012, but they had decided to come into town for my due date, even though I didn't want any guests. I assumed Livvy would come late because of my own fear, so I told my parents not to book until after she was born. Nonetheless, they came for the week I was due. I was at home watching movies and waiting out the process and trying to keep myself distant from my family. This was a season of emotional upheaval, and I was silently punishing my parents for my struggle. I hadn't known at the time that they were just part of my story and not to blame for it.

It was almost two years since David had died and Vince had an emotional affair. I was still working through my wounds, and now I had to deal with giving birth to a child. Once we were cleared to leave the hospital, Vince and I wanted to be home with Livvy, just the two of us. Vince made another sign for our driveway — "No uninvited visitors" — and locked the gate. It was nearing the time for my parents to return to Hawaii, and they hadn't seen Livvy yet. So we scheduled a time around

Memorial Day weekend for my sister's family and my parents to come over and meet Livvy Lou.

Maybe most people want their mothers during this time, but I was struggling with so many fears. Why did I feel I hadn't bonded with my mother? I was having dreams of my mom chasing me, and I was trying to get away. Why couldn't I relax around her, or desire her to be close? I wanted my mom far away from me, emotionally and physically. It was exhausting trying to figure out these emotions and where they came from. Even more important, how would I bond with Livvy when I had failed to bond with my mother? Did I possess the same inability to bond that I felt my mom had? Would I see Livvy? Hear her? Would I want to meet her needs physically and emotionally? Could I? Did I have what it took to have my heart open?

I had planned to return to work full time, with Vince keeping Livvy part time. But as the days went on, I cried at the idea of leaving her. What had happened to me? She needed her mom, and I needed to be there for her, with her. I needed to nurture her. About two weeks postpartum, Livvy lay in front of me, I stared at her and began to cry.

"I can't leave you! I can't go back to work. What is wrong with me?" I said aloud.

She didn't respond. But I knew I had to talk to my boss and Vince. It seemed like an awful time to be having these feelings because I was in the process of buying the company from my boss. The plan was I would invest over time and eventually be the owner, or majority owner, of the company. It would be my boss's retirement plan and my future business. I was a businesswoman at heart and had wanted to dominate in the business world for as long as I could remember. Kids, no. Global domination, yes.

This decision would be tricky. Did I want to back out entirely and be a stay-at-home mom? Or back out partially until I knew what I wanted? This business plan had practically been handed to me. It would be ridiculous to let it go. But it wasn't resonating anymore. All I could see was Livvy's face. I knew my desire had instantly changed when she swam up my chest and looked into my eyes. This child who had been calling to me from the other side for the last few years was here, and now my plans were changing.

I knew the only right thing was to be honest and clear. I had to cancel the buyout plan, and I could work only part time. Luckily, we had hired an office assistant before my pregnancy leave. This would be a good time for her to come on full time and cover my other work. I mustered the courage to tell my bosses, a married couple, that I would need to come back part time. Things had changed, and I hadn't expected it, but I couldn't buy the business and I couldn't come back full time. It felt right.

It was hard to muster the courage, and when I finally had the conversation, I couldn't discern how my bosses felt about it. It seemed as though he was reluctant to let me out of the deal because he figured he knew better. It seemed his wife was more intuitive and could see into the future further than I even could and agreed to the plan right away. Time would tell more.

For now, though, I was still on pregnancy leave, and I cherished every moment at home with Livvy. Vince had just finished finals for the spring semester and was able to take some family leave with us during this time. For once things seemed right. But I knew change was on the horizon.

Sleep was a challenge — for Vince and me and Livvy. For me it was worse. Although my autoimmune exhaustion had seemed to taper off during my pregnancy, it was creeping back as my hormones began to return to normal. In addition, my own childhood fears around sleep and the dark crept in, too. I hovered over Livvy, wondering if she was afraid, if she could sense when I was away from her while she slept. I wondered if she was developing bonding wounds during her infancy.

I am not sure if anyone can relate to this seemingly irrational fear, but it was intense for me. I would imagine dropping her in the driveway or onto sharp rocks. I imagined me hurting her in ways I could never, and would never, hurt her. I felt psychotic on some days and would just worry and pray the images would go away. Did other people struggle with thoughts like these? Were these more generational memories like the one from Aunt Alpha? Had these abusive things happened in my heritage somewhere, sometime unbeknownst to me?

I didn't dare tell anyone about these thoughts, not even Vince. I didn't know at the time that they were fairly common and less about me and more about my darkness. But when you don't know that, why risk getting locked up for insanity? Just keep it inside. I knew how to do that. I would continue doing my best, hoping Livvy didn't pick up on my occasional psychosis and praying it would pass.

Chapter 18

BONDING

Then there were moments I could see the future and the past when I looked into Livvy's eyes. All my fears would pass; I felt the calm after the storm. I sensed I was bonding with Livvy. I intentionally made it my goal — daily. I would look into her eyes until peace came over me. I would pass through my intimacy fears, through the unknowns in my past, and into the deepness of her soul. Then I would smile and kiss her repeatedly while she squirmed. I would say, "One hundred kisses," and kiss all over her face. She loved it. As an infant she smiled, and as she grew older, she giggled. She smiled in anticipation every time my eyes got big and I leaned in and said, "One hundred kisses." She still loves it.

Livvy was still too little to enjoy any benefits of Daddy's music industry job, but she and I would still occasionally tag along to hang out with Vince backstage, since it was usually too loud to keep a newborn near the concert fans. Livvy's first concert (not in utero) was interestingly Def Leppard, the group I did the drumming with in Topanga when I was pregnant. Unimpressed and wearing sound-canceling earmuffs, she fell asleep during the show.

Vince was working a concert at a venue in San Diego and some friends of ours really wanted tickets. Vince did his usual. He got them backstage passes and stage side seats to watch the show. If you like music, it's a blast being friends with someone in the music industry. Livvy and I tagged along this time, too. We hung around for dinner backstage and during the sound check. But once the concert started, we slipped away to the abandoned catering room so I could feed her.

The opening band came on, and I recognized its name —Thirty Seconds to Mars. I knew one of their songs very well because it was a theme song for an event I had coordinated, and where I first met Vince, in 2009. The theme song was "Vox Populi," which means "Voice of the People." My event, Justice Day, was to promote awareness of human trafficking, and "Vox Populi" had the perfect lyrics for our theme. I must have listened to that song a hundred times when planning Justice Day. I didn't know anything else about Thirty Seconds to Mars, except an unforgettable photo I had seen of their lead singer, Jared Leto. He had remarkable blue eyes.

As the music began, I strolled back into the catering room and found a small table for Livvy and me. Summertime was ending, and she was almost four months old. My breastfeeding shyness had well worn off, and I would feed her anywhere I felt inclined. I had a feeding bonding ritual: I would feed her and then lay her down so she could look at me, and I would just talk with her. I would just lay her on any table wherever we were so she could look up at me and engage. I didn't make those silly baby noises (although I do that now to both babies and dogs) but would talk in my normal voice, like she could understand and one day be able to reply intelligibly. She gazed back at me with sincerity and understanding, though never saying a thing. It was like living with a foreign exchange student who didn't speak any English but gazed with sincerity, hoping to one day communicate fully.

I fed her with the sound of the concert still in earshot but not loud enough to startle her without the earmuffs. I heard the encore song and the crowd shouting and clapping — time for a set change. I didn't even know who the next band was, or at least it hadn't registered with me enough for me to care. Our friends were still out front with Vince, and I surmised they would stay for the entire show. I was comfortable, and clipping up my bra, while Livvy lay looking up at me. Maybe I was asking her when she would be ready to head home. "Should we stay for the whole show? Hit the road? Whaddya think, kiddo? Want to find Daddy and say goodbye?" She just stared back at me, the most precious human being I had ever seen.

Just then three guys walked in and interrupted us. The one leading the way focused on us. Maybe he was surprised to find someone in the dimly lit room, or perhaps we startled him. I glanced up to acknowledge them while still adjusting my nursing bra and then went back to talking to Livvy. Livvy didn't care who they were; she was listening and looking at Mommy. The guy in the lead came closer, right into our space, and peered down into Livvy's eyes. He paused in silence and tilted his head for his eyes to align with hers. It was as if he had never seen a baby before.

His pause made me pause. Did he see the same wonder in her eyes that I saw? Then, without taking his eyes off her, he motioned and said, "Guys, come check out this baby. Look at the way she's looking at her mama! That's amazing. That's the most amazing bond I've ever seen!"

The other two quickly joined behind him but weren't as impressed as he was. Silent shrugs and casual eye rolls. Maybe it was their lack of response to his amazement, or his own pause for reflection, but he instantly retreated as if he had intruded.

"Oh my. I am so sorry for interrupting you. This is beautiful. I am so sorry. We will get outta here." He took one step back out of our space while he looked at me and made an "excuse me, ma'am" nod and smile.

When our eyes locked, I knew I had seen them before. I was looking into the eyes of Jared Leto! The three disappeared toward the buses. I sat in awe. I had achieved a bond with Livvy that made traffic stop for a high-energy rock star. The same man who wrote the song, "Vox Populi," the theme song for when I was fighting for human trafficking awareness. The theme song on the day I met Vince. This guy stopped to notice the bond between me and Livvy!

Dots connecting. Circles forming. The plot was thickening. I was finding my way.

Chapter 19

SLEEPING FEAR

Though my bond with Livvy was growing, I struggled with fear of the dark and sleep. More specifically, I projected my fear of the dark and sleep onto her. I couldn't imagine her not being afraid because my own fear was so pervasive. Patterns are so tough to break, and I engaged in them so unknowingly and robotically. I wanted to be aware of the patterns, mostly so I didn't repeat them and cause my brokenness to become Livvy's. But my story was still lurking in the dark.

I made some time to journal. I was devoted to healing and connecting. Where had my self-hatred and mistaken identity originated? Was it mine to own apart from my heritage? There is the term self-made man. I can't see how this statement can be true. Families are so interconnected and often enmeshed. The saying "The apple doesn't fall far from the tree" and the terms family demons and skeletons in the closet seemed more appropriate when describing the human condition, or particularly, my family. All I could do was keep journaling my story and asking myself the deeper question. "If the pretty story I was told was true, why do I feel so sick and disconnected from it?" Layers were coming off, but it was a tough process of swinging back and forth between what was real and what I had told myself was real. This was not a straightforward process.

On one of my meditative days, I had pulled back enough layers that a memory came flooding in. I was four or five years old, and I was in the kitchen talking to my mom. I was near the staircase that went down into the basement, where my bedroom was. I saw something moving slowly down the staircase. It seemed to pause and taunt me for a moment before proceeding down the staircase into the basement. Shivers went down my spine, and the hair on my neck stood up. I looked at my mom to see if she had seen it, but she was busy unpacking groceries, halfway listening to me, unaware even that I had stopped talking, and definitely hadn't noticed the shadow figure descending the staircase.

I tried to push further into this memory to find more of what it meant. I recognized it was in the same time frame as when I had been molested by my female babysitter. My parents had left me and my sisters with a stranger for a few days while they traveled to California to see if we would move there. My memories of that time are vague, but I do remember the babysitter touching me. One night while she was with us, I was scared and wet myself. She scolded me and took me alone to my room and took off all my clothes and touched my privates. I recall her doing something to herself, too. At the time I didn't understand what it was; now I realize she was masturbating.

My parents were very busy people. I don't recall ever playing with them, and I certainly never felt heard by them. So that day in the kitchen, I think it was after they got back from California, as I watched my mom unpack the groceries, I wanted to confide in her about what had happened, but all I felt was fear. And that is when I saw the dark shadow figure go down the staircase toward my bedroom.

Because this memory of the staircase shadow, of the molestation, and of my fear of confiding in my mom in the kitchen came flooding back to me as a result of my trying to understand my fear surrounding nighttime and sleep and the dark and parenting, I silently asked how these things were connected. The answer came rushing in, as if it had been waiting for me to ask: I was remembering the fear of the molestation. I was remembering the fear that had overwhelmed me when I was down in that room. I was remembering the fear of not being heard if I told my mom about what had happened.

My whole being felt permeated with terror. I felt unprotected. I felt betrayed. Abandoned. Again. My birth father had abandoned me while I was still in my mother's womb; my mom had abandoned me to the babysitter. But how could I blame my parents? The answer: I couldn't. They were doing their best.

Could I validate myself without blaming my mom and dad? Could I validate little Bethany, who was afraid and alone, whose innocence was taken? The answer was no. I didn't know how to do that. I resorted to tears and more fear. I gave energy to the wrong parts of myself.

The fear of being alone and victimized was running the show, and I made decisions based on this fear — for myself and for Livvy. I was the puppet, and the puppet master was fear. It would take hours to get Livvy to sleep at night. If she made a peep, I was up to attend to her. I was operating from terror. I think she knew it. She wanted to see peace in my eyes. She wanted to know everything would be okay. But I couldn't provide that at night; it wasn't inside me to give. I had one consolation. During daylight, I could relax and parent from a place of connection and intentionality. But it seemed so incongruent with what I experienced at night.

When Livvy reached five months old, Vince felt she needed to move from the baby side sleeper near my side of the bed to her own room. For the record, he was right, but at the time I didn't like him one bit for the suggestion. Tears streamed down my face. How could he be so cruel? She needed me! I hadn't known it at the time, but I needed her — a completely backwards way to parent.

I had to take consolation in the fact that Vince wasn't living in a state of fear and didn't have his own issues around nighttime or sleep. I concluded it was probably important for me to trust him and his love for Livvy and his concern for her well-being. I refused to like it, though, and I said so adamantly.

I made her room comfortable with a night-light. I set up an audio player for a repeating playlist with instrumental hymns. I left her door open, and I set her crib where I could see the edge from my side of the bed. It was all I could do to allow her to sleep in her room . . . all . . . the . . . way . . . down . . . the . . . hall. (It was probably only thirty feet away.) The first night we laid her down, I prayed for her — my best darn fearful mother prayer — and lay next to her crib, patting her back until I could hear her little snore. When I returned to my bed, I lay there holding Vince's hand while tears ran down my cheeks and soaked my pillow. I was a scared little girl wondering what the night would bring. Would I be safe? Was the shadowy figure going to visit? This went on, I want to say for days or weeks or months, but it was years.

Every night since the first night did get better, and my tears stopped, but the fear was there every time I put Livvy to sleep. Each night I would set up the room. Each night I would lie beside her and pat her back until she was asleep. Each night I would feed her once or twice and would barely sleep deep enough to rest. This night routine was wrecking me.

As time went on, sleep became a greater necessity for me. I was exhausted and figured I could nap when Livvy napped. Some days that worked, but one day she decided she would transition down to one nap — without consulting me first. Try as I did, she wouldn't go to sleep. Since I could not leave her side until she was peacefully sleeping, I was moving into deep exhaustion. On the verge of tears, I packed up Livvy and drove. Maybe she would fall asleep in the car.

Completely disheveled, I drove to Vince's work. I grabbed Livvy's diaper bag and car seat (her in it) and walked into the shop and set her at his feet.

"I need sleep. I can't do this anymore," I said.

Vince's face was pure confusion. Was I leaving him — and Livvy?

"Where are you going?" he asked.

"Home to sleep. Please don't come home," I said already walking away.

Tears rolled down my face in defeat. After my nap, I decided I needed a sleep therapist. I am laughing at myself now (I said I would laugh at that one day). There are people who make an income by advising struggling parents (like me) on how to get their baby to sleep. Vince was apprehensive about spending money on this, but he dared not interrupt my plan.

The online therapist created a customized plan for Livvy. It was really for me. Livvy didn't have a problem. The problem was mine. Implementing the plan was a struggle. It seemed that trying to change my behavior without changing the "why" behind it was useless. Day in and day out I would try to apply the advice the therapist suggested. Two weeks into it, I was in a shame spiral, out five hundred bucks, and back to ground zero. I guessed the sleep issues would be my fate.

Chapter 20

INTIMACY

Although it was hard to connect with Vince intimately during this time of pure exhaustion, it wasn't all baby related. The shadowy figure of fear around my molestation seemed to have opened Pandora's box. Although I had tucked that memory away, I was wearing the symptoms. I had in the past, and up until now, taken pride in the fact that I had always pleasured my partners sexually. I would even sometimes socially brag about this fact. Not my proudest moments but my reality. I told Vince that he should be happy that I never withheld sex and was sexually explorative. He didn't complain. But I would justify myself, as if to defend my position (no pun intended).

There was something missing I hadn't noticed before or had even cared about — connection. Not connection again! Disconnection was now creeping into my sex life. That had never been a problem before. I was a sexual person. I knew that. I had dirty thoughts and perverted jokes. The way guys at a bar (or out on the road with Vince) talked, didn't bother me. But now I was asking myself if I was being honest about my sexuality. And I had new questions about my sexual relationship with Vince. Who were we? What had we not been honest about? How could this topic escape any conversation between us?

Vince and I began slowly rolling out the sexuality conversation. What was our goal and motivation for our intimacy? Just pure physical contact? I hadn't been shy about my body. I would give Vince boudoir photos as birthday gifts. I even made him a magazine one year. In the same way, I wasn't shy about proselytizing my theories on masturbation. I wrote an article for a skater magazine on the topic of female masturbation (something I forgot I had done, but there it is). This feministic sexuality persona was part of my identity.

But now I wondered if the motivation for my behavior was to perform, or worse, to control. My family stories seemed to be connected somehow to these misgivings. I had shared with all the professionals I had visited Aunt Alpha's rape story and the cognitive resonance I had experienced. But I did not share with Vince the details of the voices that seemed to be connected to Aunt Alpha that have haunted me since I became sexually active. I wasn't ready to be truly intimate — not with myself and not with him, not with anyone.

To be honest, I wasn't present during sex. I was detached. It was performance-driven. From my readings during pregnancy, I found out that detachment is a true symptom of sexual trauma. I controlled the situation and then detached to cover the darkness. I would do the Wizard of Oz trick — "Look over here. Don't look behind the curtain."

Vince and I were on a self-discovery journey and just happy to be having sex and touching bodies. So I can't say my emotional disconnect was affecting our relationship. Yet it was an immature love, and we were okay with that.

As the intimacy topic resurfaced, however, so did the voices that said "Your father sent me in here," the voices that told me I was inherently bad and dirty. The difference was that now I could actually feel myself detaching during sex, whereas, before, I had no awareness of it. I had been on autopilot — it would happen and then it would be over. But as I became more aware that I was detaching, the more it seemed to terrorize me. Was I really in control of this? Was I doing this on purpose to protect myself? Was detaching a protection mechanism? Rising voices of confusion began inhibiting my goal of intimacy with Vince.

I looked back at each sexual relationship I had had for a pattern in hopes this wasn't surfacing with Vince just because of our marital issues. But there indeed was a pattern — fear of relationship intimacy. Fear of not being good enough to keep a man around, to be loved. I performed. I had to be what they needed, what I thought they needed. If a guy didn't stay around, I would try harder with the next guy. What did they need me to be? I started feeling like the song "Hand Me Down" by Matchbox Twenty.

What a mind game I played. Was I disconnecting to control my demons, to keep the shadowy figure from bothering me? I cried reliving each relationship, each time I had hidden myself away in order to be sexual and desirable. The pain of my hustle was bubbling up. I wanted to be someone, to keep someone. To be loved. To be worthy of love. But the fantasy of how I wanted each romance to play out couldn't be sustained in my imagination. I played the harlot. The smart, industrious, independent woman who didn't need a man. In return, each guy treated me with that understanding. They would use me and leave me. I was reinforcing my pseudo-self with each relationship, and my truth and pain were retreating further inward with festering self-hate and mistaken identity.

Chapter 21

OLD PATTERNS

This first year of mothering was packed full of Bethany-learning moments. I took some of them to heart; some I could not absorb — at that time. Truth is, time flies, and it was now the summer of 2015. Every passing day caused me to realize I did not want to continue working in real estate. I wanted to be home with Livvy. Vince was doing a great job with her, and I loved the foundation we were building for her. During that first year, both Vince and I worked part time and spent the other part of our day with Livvy.

I was hypervigilant about doing the best, most natural things we could do for Livvy. Delayed cord clamping, check. Breastfeeding, check. Whole foods, check. Outdoor nature time, check. Limited EMFs, check. We had switched away from wireless connection in the house and even went to flip phones so we weren't consumed with devices. We switched our home diet to mostly whole foods and spent a lot of time in parks and the zoo and museums. We were trying to be intentional for Livvy, and even for ourselves. I was becoming a hippie mama who was slowly melding into the woo-woo world of inner connection. *Slowly* being the operative word.

With all these changes and soul-searching, my work life was starting to unnerve me in small ways. I realized that just as I had based my relationships with men on my need to be accepted and loved, I had chosen bosses this way, too. I was magnetized to men who might love and accept me in the way I never received from my own fathers. I was learning so much about my patterns and decided working for a father figure would continue to be unhealthy for me. I would keep hustling to please him. I would undervalue myself and my time for him. It wasn't working for me anymore.

After Livvy was born, I had made that leap to part time and canceled the business buyout plan. In trying to figure out how I could still achieve my professional goals in order to dominate in the business world, I started to realize those were goals for someone who was hustling for approval. Did I still want that for myself?

At this time a former client reached out to me and scheduled a lunch meeting to discuss a proposed business venture. Livvy and I walked downtown to a local microbrewery. Matt sat in the back waiting for us. He and his wife had been property management clients of mine, and I had sold them their first house. They were now contemplating new business ventures. Matt liked my style and knowledge of real estate so much that he figured I might make a good business partner. At the time, his plan sounded promising. I would work part time at my current office and part time from home building a business that would eventually let me work from home full time.

"I know business systems; you know real estate," Matt said.

"I think I could balance this. Sounds like this aligns with my current goal of being home and available for Livvy," I replied.

"Let's start drafting up some ideas of how it would look and connect again," he proposed.

"Sounds great. I want to make sure we don't infringe on my boss's business here in town, so we need to have another service area," I asserted.

I know real estate law and that competition is the crux of keeping real estate pure at heart. Antitrust laws prohibited me from creating a service area separate from my current boss's area, but I wanted nothing more than to respect him while I ventured forth over the next few years. It would be a delicate balance, and I would have to give him a heads-up. It was the right thing to do. After all, I was appreciative of everything he had taught me, although it was not the way I would conduct my own business.

My boss had been like a dad to me. For all intents and purposes, I was part of his family. I kept thinking that I had already been abandoned by own birth father, I didn't want my boss to do the same thing to me. I wasn't sure I could cope with that. Sure, I cared more about my boss than myself, my own needs and wants. I had been through a lot since David's passing. I was going through a lot still. I wanted to keep the love I had earned from my boss. I needed it. It gave me a sense of belonging. I wish I knew then what I know now.

"I need to talk to you about some changing plans," I said reluctantly to him one day, my heart pounding out of my chest.

"What's up?" Maybe he thought I wanted back into the buyout plan now that Livvy was getting older.

"I am going to start a side business with Matt," I quickly said.

"What? What kind of side business? When will you have time for that?" he questioned.

The words "a real estate business" bolted from my mouth.

"A what?" he asked in frustration, not wanting an answer.

"We will only work the coast, out of your service area," I replied quickly, overlooking the antitrust laws I swore to myself I wouldn't bring up.

He wasn't having it anyway. The boundaries on business didn't matter; I could have left that part out. All he heard was he would eventually lose his best employee, whom he had groomed to buy his business. He would lose his retirement plan. He would lose someone he thought of as a daughter, who he thought would never leave him. I knew him well enough to know that he would angrily exit through the back door and take some time to calm down. I was right.

It would be a couple of weeks before he asked more questions about the business with Matt. And in the meantime, Matt was busy planning our next steps and crafting business plans and corporate bylaws. I hadn't needed my boss's permission, but I sure did want it. For the time being, I would walk on eggshells and work my butt off in an attempt to keep the status quo of my worth in the workplace — and in his heart.

Chapter 22

THE PENDULUM

In the telling of my process . . . journey . . . story, I recognized this very real pendulum swing that was happening during these years of discovery. Losing my first love, David, through divorce and then his passing away and then going through a marriage crisis with Vince really drove me to the end of myself. Or almost to the end of myself. I was hovering around the edges. I could see this confusing chasm, vacillation, emotional and mental, even physical at times, between the way things really were and the illusion I had told myself about how I was raised. I was pulling back the curtain to expose the façade. This illusion was tall, sturdy, and built to stand.

Would I keep my agreement with the family system or break away from it? Breaking away to choose a healthier path would mean more rejection, or better put, facing the fear of rejection. Committing to the broken family system meant I could continue being accepted by the people in the system. Broken or whole, it was a system. There was belonging in the lack of belonging. There was connection in the disconnection.

We may have been going through the motions, but we were doing it together as a unit.

There is the "but" in the story — I was a part of that dysfunctional unit. For me, there had to be a breaking away, a tearing apart, and a real recognition that the system didn't fit me anymore. I realized that if I wanted a different way, I had to face the fear of rejection and abandonment, real or imaginary. Rejection and abandonment were part of my deepest pain and the reasons why I vacillated between embracing the truth or staying within the system as it was.

I deeply desired connection and the truth of my story to bring light into my darkness. I was part of a broken family dynamic that had been plugging along well before I entered earth. Who was I to break away and expose the system?

I didn't want to expose anyone, especially not my family, whom I deeply wanted to please, and whom I deeply wanted to accept and love me. Upset the apple cart? No! Rock the boat? Nope. I didn't want the skeletons in the closet to have a light shone on them. By God, if the apple was going to fall, it shouldn't fall far from the tree (I guess that's enough metaphors to describe it — I am laughing at myself)!

The pendulum would swing. I wanted to connect to the pain inside me with a true story. A story that resonated, one that pointed toward healing. My pain wasn't created in a vacuum and did not pop out of thin air. Yet, the more I looked at the image my family portrayed, the more I convinced myself it wasn't just an image, it was real. I must be the bad egg. So I would shrink back to seeing my issues were mine alone.

We can paint pretty pictures to believe in, or we can commit to venturing into the attic, or in my case the staircase into the basement. To say the least, I was a basket case. On an emotional roller coaster. Not only was I acting completely incongruently, I was feeling the ups and downs, too. I was living the song "Sick Cycle Carousel" by Lifehouse, just wanting to step down from it all.

It was during this process of healing that I realized my behavior had been on this roller coaster for much longer than I was ready to admit. When I was married to David he had described my inconsistent behavior to a psychotherapist who had concluded I was suffering from a type of bipolar disorder. The little Bethany inside wanted nothing more than to belong, to be seen and heard. I had been suffering for a very long time and yet quieted the longing inside me. The longing was still there, crying from the depths of my soul.

I wanted to lean into my mother's embrace and feel at home there. Could I be seen and heard for who I was and not who she hoped I would be to meet her needs? I wanted my father to want me. To stay around. To call and express his pride in my being. I wanted to be free to be me. I wanted to be validated. I wanted these things, and I didn't even know what they meant. When the longing inside me could not be quieted, I would perform. You want funny? I will be funny. You want smart? I will be brilliant. You want results? I will overproduce. I wrote this in my journal in September

2015 while navigating my way through this muck and mire:

I couldn't remember what I believed today. How do I feel about hugs? I have been "huggy" for the "huggy people." I even say everyone needs to hug and people who don't have issues. Then I turn around and say, "I'm not really a hugging person" with people who aren't into hugging.

Do I like hugs? What is the popular opinion on hugs?

Sometimes I don't tell the truth. I will tell half the story because I don't want to divulge all the information. There are only a handful of people who get full disclosure — or do they? Am I just pretending I am connected to "some people" when I don't think I even grace myself with full disclosure?

I have to remember who I am for each person. But then I forget what I was. I can't keep that up. Talk politics with these people, but don't with them. Forget who I am supposed to be with who and then say the wrong things in the wrong group and come off judgmental. This is even confusing me. What am I even talking about? Who am I really?

Could I pull myself together and find who I was instead of who I thought I needed to be for acceptance and love?

Chapter 23

ENMESHMENT

I was homeschooled from second grade until I went to college. A little fun fact: My mom enrolled me in college classes to supplement classes at home when I was just eleven years old. By fifteen I had taken the State of California's high school exit exam and joined the student body at my community college. I was that awkward homeschooled kid walking around campus with a fuzzy yellow backpack.

Shortly after my sixteenth birthday I earned my associate degree and was the college's youngest degree holder at that time. My mom earned her associate degree at the same time I did. We have a photo of both of us, each in our cap and gown, holding our diplomas on graduation day. Enmeshed much?

In retrospect, homeschooling did save me from having to choose how I wanted to fit in If I had gone to public school — boy chaser or teacher's pet? Being stuck at home and aiming to please just my mother sheltered me from a lot of the social anxieties of belonging and bullying. Yet having only my mother to please wasn't always healthy for me. Luckily, I didn't know about this struggle at the time — not consciously, anyway.

During grade school, I loved homeschooling, but when I got older, I cautioned anyone who thought about it as an option. I hated it. I blamed it — and church — for my sheltered upbringing and family dysfunction. But now, knowing what I do, I can't say homeschooling is all bad. If done right, homeschooling may actually be the way to go for kids these days. It was actually my broken family system in the context of homeschooling that made it tough for me and my emotional health. Then again, I can never know what might have been if I had gone to public school. I just don't blame homeschooling anymore.

Only in recent years have I come to appreciate the sacrifices my parents made to homeschool. There are so many good things I didn't realize about my parents while I was unwinding the hard pain of my story. I don't think I could have, or even should have. If I had, I would have kept using the good bits to cover the bad and invalidate the reality of my story. I ended up doing that enough anyway.

My mom and I had been enmeshed with each other for many, many years, so it seemed only logical that she would be upset by my getting married and moving to Australia. She was losing me, and I desperately wanted to get lost. David was my way out. I did love David in the deepest way that I was capable of at the time, but I didn't know to what extent my desire to get away was intertwined with my love for him until much later in life.

My mom and I got into a big fight the week before my wedding. I was upset with her up until the day of the wedding. I didn't even want her in the dressing room before my nuptials. She came in for a brief moment while I was dressing, and we exchanged some harsh words. My sisters kicked her out of the room. The day after my wedding, I flew with David to Australia, where he attended college. I hardly spoke to my mom for that year. The way I tell it, she never called or cared about me while I was away. Neither of my fathers bothered to connect with me, either, while I was overseas. My version of this story was exaggerated in my mind because of my own issues — I was alone and truly abandoned. No checks and balances on this imaginary conversation.

When I returned from Australia, I kept emotional (and sometimes physical) distance from my parents. Maybe it was my form of retribution, my way of punishing them for what I perceived as their lack of care, or intentionality, regarding my life. But the truth is, there was just a lot of drama between us. Drama was in the fiber of our family. There was a lot to undo and unlearn and relearn and heal. I hadn't even known it yet. Instead of connecting to my feelings, which I didn't know how to do then, I did the most rebellious thing a good, Christian, homeschooled girl could do — I sulked and pouted and behaved passive aggressively.

My mom inquired about my behavior. She didn't understand my cold responses. I didn't understand my cold responses. I just felt pain and rejection and betrayal in all the areas of my soul. I didn't know how to express my hurt because I had no training. Lord knows she didn't know how to express herself in a healthy way. My mom is the queen of reactive behavior, giving in to knee-jerk reactions. Who knew you could actually just observe your emotions without responding to them, assess what your soul is telling you without reacting? I didn't know anything about emotional health back then. Fortunately, my mom and I have come light-years from that old behavior.

Several of our conversations ended in arguments. I never quite knew what we were arguing about, but passions swirled inside each of us. The reason for our fighting went deeper than either one of us knew, and we were trying to find the language to express it, language we didn't yet have.

Months turned into years, and then we began to make some headway. One day one of us brought up the topic of my biological father, and it created such a ruckus that it was impossible to ignore that he was the epicenter of much of the pain. This particular argument ended with a heartfelt apology and a gift. My mom showed up at my office with a dozen roses in a majestic blown-glass vase (I still have the vase standing like a trophy on my shelf, reminding me of that very difficult season of life and the ability to persevere). Her apology was as deep as it could have been with the information we had, with a lot unbeknownst to either of us at the time. These were the years the outer layers of pain were peeling off. There would be many more for both of us.

Chapter 24

FAWNING

Agony happens to us all. Struggle is said to be the pathway to growth. I would agree. It sucks swamp water, but I agree. The heartbreak of my young divorce with David and his subsequent death was the darkest period of my life. Finding out that Vince was having an emotional affair on the heels of David's death, gut-wrenching. Beginning to discover the source of my family's toxicity made my head spin. My darkness was at a whole different level and seemed outside me. It was personal but didn't feel like it was happening to me like the events with David and Vince had.

How I handled my relationships with David and Vince had everything to do with the skills I didn't have because of the unhealthy dynamics of my family structure. I didn't possess the emotional and mental strength to navigate adult relationships and tragedies from a healthy baseline.

I was opening doors to things that were pressed down and packed in darkness for decades, for generations. These secrets were the patterns I was born into. They reinforced the pain I experienced with David and Vince and caused the darkness to linger. Darkness was the reason I drastically feared having a child. The reason I felt unsafe in my skin. The reason I didn't trust myself or others. The reason I was hypervigilant and my adrenal glands were on overload.

I recently heard about the new addition to the idea of fight or flight. There are four responses now, and I actually relate most to the newest on the list. Maybe you do, too. Fight. Flight. Freeze. Fawn. The first three are familiar and fairly self-explanatory. But fawn means to become co-dependent or enmeshed to protect one's self. In order to be safe, people become what is asked of them. Whether it is emotional, mental, physical, or sexual abuse, people will submit to it for their own safety. Sounds a lot like Stockholm syndrome, when captives bond with their captor. For primal safety, I lost myself by being who, or what, I needed to be.

Well before I knew the term, I was good at fawning. The term isn't really what is important here. Safety is what I desired. We all do. Little humans grow up in preset family systems and try to find the safest path through them. That's why kids are called resilient. They have to be.

The epitome of insult to injury came as a surprise to me the month I was preparing to marry David. My parents had set the goal for me to finish my bachelor's degree before marrying, which meant doubling up on coursework — 20 units in my final semester. So I was planning a wedding, hustling with college coursework, working, and packing to move to Australia the day after my wedding. Also, my twentieth birthday was on December 9 of that year, 2000, and was followed by semester finals, Christmas, New Year's, and my wedding on January 8, 2001. This was when my dad called my older sister and me to his office for a meeting.

This meeting goes down as one of my worst memories of all time. It's in my top 5 in my timeline. Inwardly I was already struggling with feeling out of place in my family, feeling innately dirty and bad. I had to keep it cool and "fawn" for the parents who were struggling with their own issues surrounding the topic of my mom's former marriage and my adoption.

Sitting in the two seats across from my dad's oversized desk, my sister Heather and I wondered why we had been summoned.

"I called you here because Bethany is about to get married and move away. I wanted to get your feedback on how I parented you," my dad said awkwardly.

What a strange request, I thought. Yet, I was angry with both my mom and dad for how I was treated after my mom introduced me to my birth father. It was only a few years prior, but nothing in our house was ever the same after that. My sisters did not want to acknowledge we actually had a blended family. They disagreed with me about my wanting to meet him and them blamed me for the disruption in the household because my parents had not dealt with their own emotions around my mom's divorce and our adoption. My parents had created a story, a façade, and they and my sisters liked it more than the truth. My parents had emotionally blackballed each other. I knew I was the problem. I had rocked the boat, and I hadn't even done it on purpose. I was born in what felt like the wrong time, the wrong family, and on the wrong continent.

I thought I could passively answer his question with a one-word reply: "Fine." Everything was fine. That's what he wanted to hear. No. He wanted to hear that it was great. He had rehearsed this in his head. He was the savior to my mom by becoming a father to me and Heather. We had been abandoned by our birth father, and he had given up his own plans in order to take us in off the street. He wanted to hear that he was the hero. But I couldn't stomach those words. I had so much rage inside me, and it wanted out. Now would be the time. I would be as non-aggressive as possible, but my words would be wounding.

"Well, you didn't molest us or anything, but it isn't a secret that you weren't necessarily there for us in ways we needed," I blurted out.

Heather spun toward me in shock, and her eyes widened in worry.

I instantly regretted my choice of words. But since I have a stubborn streak, it was too late to pull them back. So I stood by them. Fearful. But I didn't rescind them in any way. I know now that, whatever my dad needed to hear from me, he didn't deserve what I said.

He flew back with hurtful words. I can't recall them all. My sister was shouting over us to stop yelling at one another. She sobbed through her shouting. She was not okay. Neither was I, but I powered up against my dad.

"Get out! Get out of my office! Get out of my house! You are hereby disowned from my life! You are no longer my daughter! Get out!" he shouted at me.

I was not crying; I was fuming. His words shut me down, and I stormed out of his office. I made a beeline to the main road and started walking. David lived a few blocks from my dad's office. I knew I could just walk to his house (this was before cell phones). Heather pulled up alongside me at the stoplight. She was bawling. She yelled at me to get in the car. I shook my head. The light turned green, and she pulled away. I crumbled in tears as I fumbled my way the few blocks to David's.

I knocked on his door, and he was startled to find such a blubbering mess on his porch. He was at a loss for words. I needed him to take me to my parents' house so I could pack up the rest of my things. The wedding was just weeks away, and most of my stuff was already packed. He wasn't sure leaving my parents' house like that was a good idea. But there was no other option. My dad had just disowned me. I was fatherless. Completely demoralized.

He took me home. My sister was not there, but my mom met us in the driveway. She begged me to apologize. What had Dad said to her? Apologize? It was over. I was there to pack and go.

David pulled me aside.

"Maybe just apologize. We are leaving in less than a month. We can't leave like this. We can deal with it all later," he said.

I saw the uncertainty in his face. There was fear, too. This was all too familiar and triggering his own wounds. He didn't know how to support me. He wanted it all to be okay.

This was the moment. This was the very minute I chose. I remember it cognitively. If you pretend, if you say what they need to hear, if you do what they need, you can push it all down and away. You can stop feeling, and you can be invincible. So I took a deep breath and became a robot. I followed David and my mom into the house. My dad was sitting at the head of our kitchen table, his face filled with anger and sadness. It didn't matter. I didn't need to respond to his feelings.

I sat down at the other end. David and Mom sat on either side of the table between us. I took another breath.

"I am sorry for what I said," I said as if I were a robot.

I can't even remember if I looked at him. Most likely I did, my face like a stone. Strong and immovable. Machine-like. Nothing would be quite the same. For me. For my heart. For quite some time.

Although I know now that struggle is essential for growth, it seems that, for growth to happen, the person struggling must be aided by the presence of a kind caregiver who can help them navigate age-appropriate challenges without rescuing them. Subsequently, when rupture happens in a relationship, there is repair and restoration through conversation. Instead, this situation, and many others, was detrimental to me. I had no training in how to navigate my challenges. There were no healthy caregivers along the way. Trauma caused more harm and shame. There were no tools in my belt for interpersonal relationships. But, then again, my parents didn't have them either.

Chapter 25

DECISIONS

After I had announced to my boss in the summer of 2015 that I would be starting a side business, life around the office was like walking on eggshells. My boss made several attempts to change my mind. He proposed new ideas every few days to try to convince me not to start my own business. He also attempted to get me back into the original buyout plan with him. When those efforts didn't work, he created other investment opportunities, hoping one might pique my interest, and my pocketbook.

In spite of his efforts, I never relented. I wanted my new opportunity. It made sense to me for Livvy, for my future, in ways his opportunities didn't. I also felt a rebellion rising up in me to get away from another father figure. A need to be on my own, to learn to trust myself and make some of my own decisions. I knew I would never be independent working for him. Although I would have loved for that to have been possible, I had to shake off and shake out of the role I had put myself into.

The long Labor Day weekend was approaching, and I would have three days to spend with Vince and Livvy, and I was happy for the break. The Friday afternoon before the holiday, my boss came through the office, and he wasn't happy. I could tell. We all could tell. He made some comment that I should use the weekend to decide where I wanted to work. I took his bark as an ultimatum. It brought up those memories with my dad before my wedding many years before. What would happen next?

I spent the time on the drive home playing out imaginary conversations with Vince. I don't recall if I spoke out loud or if they were all in my head. I rehearsed all the ways I could explain to Vince that I would not be starting a new business after all. What would he say and how would I respond? I rationalized why it would be best to just stay and not upset the apple cart. There was no other option than to back out of the new deal with Matt and opt for a stable income, to please my boss. I had to. It would be too iffy for me to back out of my steady paycheck, especially with a child.

After much consideration, I decided to lead the conversation with the statement my boss made. Maybe that would just be all I needed to say, and Vince would come to the same conclusion I had. I did. He did not.

"Easy decision. Quit," Vince said.

"Quit what?" I asked in confusion.

"Quit your job. You have been working all summer to create a corporation with Matt. That's where our future is, not with the job you have now." He took a decided stance.

"What about a steady paycheck? Safety net? You're not even working full time," I rationalized in fear.

"It doesn't make any sense to keep going when you can break out and do something for yourself. It's an easy decision. You start this, and I will go back full time," he replied.

This was one more time I figured I should trust Vince's judgment. He wasn't in the same toxic head space I was in. My people-pleasing patterns were bound to dominate if I let them.

I didn't know how I could actually look my boss in the eye and tell him I had made my decision and it wasn't to stay with him. This wasn't going to be easy. I was a small child on the inside, and disappointing this person wasn't something I could do. It wouldn't go well, and I already was feeling the sting of rejection. With that I mind, I figured I would just quit via text or a letter. Coward's way out, I know. I chose a letter.

Since it was a long weekend, I thought I could just leave the letter on his desk and wait for him to read it on Tuesday and avoid direct confrontation. Confrontation I could not stomach. So I sneaked into the office over the weekend and left my resignation on his keyboard. On Tuesday, his wife got there before he did, discovered the letter, and decided to read it herself before anyone else came in. By the time I arrived, I knew she had called him, and her face showed she had been crying. She gave me a consoling hug and an understanding look that said she knew I was doing what was best for me and Livvy Lou. She didn't have words because she was holding back her tears. Which brought tears to my eyes. We both knew what would come once her husband arrived. We waited and walked on eggshells together.

As I recall, he showed up very late that day, no doubt trying to calm down instead of arriving in a fury. He did a halfway job with that. I don't remember many words being exchanged. He knew I was leaving, and there wasn't anything he could do about it. I imagine his wife had told him that his comment had sounded like the ultimatum that I had taken it for and that was what had pushed me out. He tried to backtrack and assure me that it wasn't an ultimatum and that I could stay. But the die had been cast, and I wasn't changing my mind. I guess even more than my feeling intimidated and small, I was stubborn.

I told him I would give him a month so I could transfer all my knowledge and files to the new girl. I wanted it to go well for him and didn't want to leave a gaping hole. I also committed to not working "his area," which was technically against the law. He didn't want me to tell any of the clients I was leaving. He also didn't want me to tell the service providers or use any of the service providers, as that would tip off clients that I had left. I committed to his rules for ease of transition. Although stubborn and determined, I was still scared of being on my own and scared of upsetting him any more than I had.

Feel Good Property Management launched. I was the broker and partner. By October I was without a steady paycheck, and Vince went back to working full time with the sound company. I played Destiny's Child's "Survivor" on repeat to encourage myself toward independence and freedom. I wanted to keep growing, and I felt like this was a big step in that direction. I was growing up — a little.

Chapter 26

MOVING HOUSE

The first few months of our new business were challenging. I did like the pace of working from home all day and being with Livvy, but I needed her to sleep. Our new property management company was growing super-fast. I was training my new partners in the real estate industry, and they were managing all our online systems. Matt had been an engineer at Apple Inc. He was a systems guy, and his systems were proving to work because our new company was growing. Business was busy, but we needed to retain the funds within the company for building the business. We decided to defer paychecks for the first twelve months.

There was one evening when Livvy wanted to breastfeed nonstop. I recall her being like a demon child sucking out my life. She wasn't herself. She was especially needy and clinging and clawing. I didn't sleep that night. Writhing. Angry. The next day I told Vince I needed to quit breastfeeding. Livvy was eighteen months old, and she was very healthy. I figured it would be the only way to get her to sleep through the night. But I was terrified of inflicting on her a feeling of being abandoned if she had to sleep the whole night in her own room without breastfeeding. What a mess.

By December Vince did another intervention. His idea: I would take a Nyquil and sleep in our room with earplugs. He would sleep alongside Livvy in the other room, on the other side of the house so I could not hear her. What a plan (sarcasm). I felt awful. The earplugs and Nyquil could knock me out and keep me from hearing her cry, but I would know and feel the terror of my own projections. Vince suggested I not ask how she did without me. He knew I would cave in if I knew she struggled, and it wasn't just me who needed to sleep. Livvy needed to start sleeping well, too. Our days needed more structure. Toddlers need to know a parent is firm and kind and available, not wishy-washy and full of fear and projecting their worries onto the kiddo. That was me. It had to stop for both our sakes. I had to start facing some of the darkness. Sadly, I only knew to muscle through it; I had no other tools yet.

It took about four days with Livvy and Vince sleeping in the other room for Livvy to sleep through the night. I didn't ask more. Once Vince broke her of breastfeeding at night, he moved her back to her own room to sleep through the night within eyeshot of my side of the bed. By the fourth good night of sleep, the days started to become clearer.

As far as my new business was concerned, I was working very hard to get it off the ground. It wasn't long until I began to see relationship patterns. Had I just left one daddy figure to please another? I was the real estate expert, and the business depended on me and my license to operate. Yet it felt like I was a pawn — and I was a pawn. Fawning again for my worth. I put myself in that position. It was a game I knew and was comfortable playing.

In January we received a rent increase from our landlord, aka my former boss, (should have seen that coming). Vince and I started looking for a new place to live. It was becoming increasingly awkward being tenants of someone who wasn't fond of me. We worried if something broke or we had a service request, he might let it go unanswered. It just wasn't a good situation. I had broken up with him, and he was an unhappy ex.

With Livvy and me now sleeping well and Vince working full time, we seemed to be doing better than we had been. I liked structure. I started looking for a new house to rent. Every new rental I acquired for our business, I would suspect it to be my next house. But upon further inspection, none seemed to jive with our needs. So we made an offer to my former boss to purchase the house we lived in. We really liked it there and had lived there almost three years. He declined.

It wasn't until late spring that a prospective client contacted me about a house he wanted to rent. I thought it would work for us. It was an old house and needed work, and I could use that for leverage in getting a good rental rate. When the client signed the contract with us, I propositioned him regarding my being his tenant. All the stars lined up, and we gave our notice to move.

The new place, we called it the "red house," was musty and smelled funny. We knew it would need to be painted and freshened up. This was part of the agreement with the new landlord. We painted the whole place before we moved in. I chuckle thinking back to that time. We covered the floors in plastic, and Vince rented a paint sprayer. He had a full hazmat suit on to paint each room. It was early August and very hot. When he took the suit off, he was dripping with sweat.

By late August we were ready to move into our new place. We had a late birthday celebration for Vince with a backyard barbecue with our friends and family. This house would take time to clean up, but we felt we could be happy there. And it was only two doors down from a family that attended our church.

We figured it was time for us to get new furniture. We had always bought secondhand stuff or had hand-me-down furniture. The house was a quaint, mid-century, modern design, so now we would have the chance to select furniture that matched the look of the house. I was excited.

The house had an additional detached garage in the alley in the back. I decided I would transform this old, musty garage into my office for my new business. The first year operating the business was a hustle but proving to be a success. I would work hard all day and work on the house when I had time. I was very busy, but I felt freer than I had before. Livvy went wherever I went, including to home inspections and showings. I scheduled all my client calls for when she napped. In addition to working hard, we were meeting our benchmarks to earn a monthly income.

Over the coming weeks, Vince noticed some very strange things about the house. Although it didn't feel weird to me, I didn't feel quite right physically and emotionally. Vince suspected that the house was haunted but was cautious about sharing his feelings. He didn't want to alarm me since I was home alone most of the time with Livvy.

Apparently, there was a picture in the red house that seemed to move. Vince would place the photo facing frontwards, and the next day it would be facing the wall. He didn't want to tell me, but one day he cracked and asked if I was messing with him. I pressured him to tell me why he asked me that, and he told me that he assumed I had been moving the photo. He later reported that doors would shut on their own, too. For some reason I was not picking up on it. Needless to say, Vince was on edge living in the red house.

Chapter 27

INTRUDER

One cold night in November we were sound asleep when we awoke suddenly to the neighbor's dogs barking in rage. We heard shuffling in the leaves, and a shadow passed our bedroom window.

"Check Livvy. Call 911!" Vince barked and ran from the bedroom and down the hallway.

I ran to see if Livvy was safe. Thankfully, she was sound asleep in her bed. Had someone been in the house? Was the house secure? Where was Vince? I grabbed the phone and dialed 911 while I walked the perimeter of the inside of the house, making sure doors and windows hadn't been broken into. Then I searched for Vince. I peeked out the front window into the driveway and then walked toward the kitchen to peek out back. I heard the 911 operator pick up. Just then I saw Vince scuffling with another man. I heard shouting.

"Silencio! Abajo!" ("Shut up! Stay down!") Vince demanded, wrestling the man to the ground.

"We have a backyard intruder, and my husband is on top of him. 540 East Eighth Avenue. Please send an officer!" I barked into the phone.

"We have police units already in pursuit. Stay inside, and we will be right there," the operator assured me.

No less than sixty seconds later, twelve squad cars and SUVs came hauling up the road and surrounded our house. When I ran out to direct them to the backyard, I saw Eli, our neighbor from church. Apparently, our neighbors had heard the intruder cross their yards, too. Eli emerged from his house once he saw the squad cars. I yelled to Eli while simultaneously informing the cops: "Vince has a guy pinned down in the backyard!"

Cops ran along each side of the house. I heard banging and the cracking of the side fence as they bashed through the side with no gate. Eli was running as fast as his legs could carry him, yelling "Vinnnce!" He actually scaled the side yard retaining wall, up and over the gate and around the police.

What I hadn't told Eli or the cops, because time was of the essence, was that Vince was in his birthday suit. Vince happens to sleep in the buff. Because we had seen the shadow move past our window so fast, there was no time for Vince to dress before dashing to ensure our safety.

Vince had confronted the intruder, and the guy came after him. Vince spun him around and pulled his arms around to his back and held him to the ground with his knees on the guy's neck. The guy had been running from the cops and ran into the wrong yard! Eli and the cops were both surprised at Vince's attire — socks!

Vince handed the guy to the cops and made a wisecrack: "Dozens of officers but just one of him."

"Go get dressed!" one cop replied to Vince's snarky remark.

Eli just gave Vince a cheesy smile and a high-five.

Vince went to put some clothes on. I checked on Livvy again. Within moments we had made a short report to the cop taking notes, and then they all were gone. We were left with a broken side fence and making up our own stories about what had happened.

The next day I called the police department to find out the story on the guy who ran through our yard, but the cops would not release any details to me. The only thing they said was that they had heard about my naked husband, no mention that Vince was the one who had pinned the perpetrator down. I found that strange. But I guess that's how those things work.

The neighbors were all asking how Vince had captured the intruder. Funny stories were going around, and one neighbor called Vince the neighborhood hero without a cape, like Greek fighter without a loin cloth. I said he was the "naked caper." I had a shirt made for him with "#nakedcaper" printed on it.

While talking with me about the intruder, one of my neighbors said our house was cursed.

"Why do you say that?" I inquired.

"Everyone at that house seems to die. The last few people who lived there died strangely. One person actually committed suicide in there years ago. I didn't want to tell you," she replied.

Well, holy moly! Good to know. Since I was in real estate, I was able to look up all the previous owners. Each family who had owned the house had at least one person die while owning that house, even young people. Made sense now why doors were shutting by themselves and pictures were being moved. But what were we supposed to do about it? I kept thinking of the shadow figure on the staircase when I was five years old. I would have to find a way to make sure we didn't have bad luck in that house.

Chapter 28

SEXUAL HEALING JOURNEY

I was feeling more and more abnormal in that house. I was working a ton and had a lot of pressure with the new business and all the new clients pouring in, and I didn't feel good physically. Headaches had been a thing of the past, but they were surfacing again and were intense. I didn't realize at the time that they were migraines. They left me with memory issues and forgetfulness, and I would lose track of time and what I had done while I had the headaches. I also would forget someone's name or a word and was extremely sensitive to light. I chalked it up to being busy and stressed, an easy excuse.

Then I started feeling depressed and would often get confused and dizzy. Whatever was happening to me was making me feel crazy, but I didn't want anyone to know or worry that something was wrong with me. I tried hard to cover up my feelings with performance. Back to my old ways, I guess. Numbers with the business were growing, and my partners were not complaining, so I kept quiet. But Vince noticed.

Around this time, I contacted Aaron, my therapist, whom I hadn't seen in a few years. In fact, I hadn't seen Aaron since before Livvy was born. I made an appointment to see if he could shed light on my symptoms. Aaron figured we should pick up where we left off. Maybe my symptoms were pointing to something deeper — Aunt Alpha and the cognitive resonance of the family sexual trauma. He proposed that since I had given birth and was now raising a girl of my own that I might benefit from addressing the family trauma. He gave me a book from his shelf called The Sexual Healing Journey: A Guide for Survivors of Sexual Abuse by Wendy Maltz.

I did my best to start the book. I read a few pages, but my eyes would glaze over and the room would go dark. I felt it viscerally, specifically in my vagina and head. I felt like I would pop or explode or die. I put the book down. Wasn't this supposed to help? A few days later I would read a few more pages. The same response occurred. I felt frozen, swallowed up by the couch. The room went fuzzy, and each time I felt it in my vagina and head. I felt like I would die or wanted to die. It was very confusing. I made another appointment with Aaron to tell him about the response to the book. I brought the book with me to the appointment.

"Here's your damn book back!" I said as I tossed it on the desk.

"You didn't like it?" Half statement, half question.

"Didn't like it? It makes me want to die!" I exclaimed.

"Okay. Let's talk about it," Aaron replied calmly. "In the meantime, I will hold on to it for you."

Was this book a test to see if I needed help? To see if it would cause a reaction in me? Measure where I was in my darkness? I guess if it was a test, it worked and did show I was messed up. We jumped back into the sexual trauma therapy. Aaron suggested we try EMDR (eye movement desensitization and reprocessing), a therapeutic process that helps heal PTSD (post-traumatic stress disorder) through relieving tension by reprocessing emotional destress.

Working with Aaron would need to continue for a while, at least until I figured out why I was struggling again. Getting life under control and back to normal seemed to be my main objective. A few weeks into working with him and while trying to read the beginning of The Sexual Healing Journey, I was walking Livvy down the road in her stroller and looked up at the sky and thought, I want to die. I want to be gone. It was the darkness swirling around me, provoking me and taunting me. I checked back into reality by looking down at Livvy sleeping.

"I need help. Livvy can't lose me," I said aloud.

Back home I Googled local rehab facilities. I called a few to see how they could help. When Vince got home, I told him I should check in to a facility. I called Aaron to ask for a recommendation, and he adamantly disagreed with me (I just love this guy). He said that Livvy needed me, and leaving for rehab might cause residual issues in her. I didn't want that. He suggested that I come see him every day until I felt stable. Vince and I agreed that would be best.

Meeting with Aaron every day was helping. We kept talking and doing EMDR therapy. But I was still feeling cognitively off-balance. I decided to make an appointment with Jamie, my acupuncturist, and Liz, my chiropractor. I had stopped all non-essential expenses when we started the business because our budget was limited, and I hadn't seen either one of them in quite some time. I saw Liz first. She did muscle testing and looked at me with a serious expression.

"Something isn't right with you, Bethany," she said.

"I know, Liz," I replied sarcastically.

"It could be mold. Will you have your blood tested?" she asked.

"Sure. I will have it checked," I replied.

After visiting Liz, I went to my acupuncturist. I told her Liz's concern about mold. My acupuncturist agreed something was off and also wanted me to have my blood checked.

After seeing Jamie, I called my primary care doctor and asked to have my blood checked for mold. He asked me a series of questions regarding my allergies, my breathing, and my sinuses. Since I had none of those issues, he wondered why then I wanted to check for mold. But we always had a good relationship, and I never visited him for trivial issues. He agreed to test me for some of the major types of mold in our area. He cautioned me that there are thousands of types of mold and wasn't sure if the test would be helpful.

Days later my primary doctor called to tell me I had mold poisoning with two types of mold and that

Vince and Livvy should be tested. My levels were very high and were most likely related to my cognitive issues — headaches, memory issues, dizziness, and even the depression.

Livvy and Vince went to get checked. We waited for the results, and when they came back negative, we wondered where the mold was coming from. Was it not the house? Livvy went everywhere I went. We learned this fun fact: Someone can have a reaction to mold that other people who are exposed to it don't have. Like peanuts or animal allergies. Every person's system is vulnerable in different ways. My doctor suggested we have the house tested.

I called some companies and had the main rooms and the garage tested for the types of mold that popped up on my blood test. Sure enough, the lab results for the house came back with higher levels. My body and mind were in overwhelm trying to cope with moving, starting our new business, healing sexual trauma, and suffering an allergy to the two types of mold.

It was December and we had been in the house for almost four months. We had finally bought our new furniture, painted the house, and began settling in. But now we had to get out of our lease. I had to tell my partners and my landlord/clients about the mold poisoning and find a new place to live. I needed help in so many ways.

Chapter 29

SPINNING OUT

My parents offered us their guest room to stay in — the same room I had lived in when David and I split up. Wow, that was trippy. Thankfully, my pastor offered the church college team to pack and move our belongings to storage. We exited the red house more quickly than we had entered. Livvy, Vince, and I moved into my parents' spare room, where we stayed while I continued with Aaron and rode out my mold poisoning. I was (and still am) thankful for all the times by parents offered their help in time of need. This time they literally saved my life. Although it felt counterproductive to me to be there while I was in the throes of processing my family trauma with Aaron, it was a place to recuperate, and I was so grateful.

In addition to working with Aaron on trauma, a spiritual guidance minister at my church suggested I try an inner healing program. She explained that inner healing was less psychological and more spiritual in nature. I had been raised in church and was guarded about spiritual healing groups. They were the reason I was hesitant about seeking further spiritual answers. I had checked the box "Done that" for years in the church of my childhood, where I had learned to play the age-old, fake-it-till-you-make-it game. Those ways were not working for me anymore. I no longer bought the straitlaced approach that if I was struggling, it was my fault because I had sinned.

But I liked the spiritual guidance minister at my new church and trusted her suggestion. I figured it couldn't hurt at this point to check it out. Unfortunately, the inner healing pastor that the spiritual guidance minister referred me to had just retired. Lucky for me, she would still see people who were in precarious situations who were referred to her. So I met with the inner healing pastor, Pastor Clarke, and though she didn't have an office anymore, she agreed to weekly meetings in her living room.

In all my years in church, chasing God for approval, I had never seen the inner healing material that she offered. I had, at one time, read similar books and had attended a seminar that reflected some of the material, but it was nothing quite like this material.

In my church growing up, I had tried my darnedest to do all the "church things" and performed to play the part. I prayed, worked in the nursery, cleaned the church, volunteered hours, and served the community. I was the good, homeschooled church-attending girl who pursued God (secretly hoping it would rid me of filth and torment). But try as I did, I did not find freedom, and I wanted it desperately.

I thought I was banging on the right doors. Turns out it was mostly an exercise in futility. The church I was raised in was full of people just as confused as I was, including, and especially, the pastor. "Just go to more church services," "volunteer more," "pray louder," "worship harder," "sit closer to the front" and everything might work out for you (on the outside). Shoot, I dominated that lifestyle. I learned it and retaught it and proselytized it. It was my jam. I hated jam.

The inner healing work presented to me now seemed very odd. It wasn't like the work I had done before, the pastor's ministry. It was work on me. Much like the work Aaron had asked me to do, it was giving myself a lot of attention, which felt foreign, maybe even selfish and wrong. It also seemed to unlock more of Pandora's box, like The Sexual Healing Journey book. I was unearthing the darkness.

Pastor Clarke had me start with notes about my family. How did I feel about my father? How did he treat my mother? Did he take responsibility for the family? Did he protect and provide for me? Then she asked me questions about my mother and questions about relationships with significant people in my life, including my sisters. The questions even went farther up my family tree, asking for personality traits and addictions and spiritual practices of older family members. These were very strange questions that no one had ever asked me. They caused me to sit and ponder more of what I had started asking years before. All of it uncovered more uncertain feelings and thoughts. Did these things play a vital role in my health?

Over the next few months, while at my parents, I continued with the inner healing work, kept on with Aaron, and had my blood levels checked periodically to ensure they were stabilizing from the mold. In the midst of this, Vince and I were looking for a house for ourselves. We looked to buy or rent; it didn't matter. Since the real estate market was strong, making offers on houses was tough in our limited price range. We made offers, but nothing was ever accepted. In March my parents' neighbor informed us that a house in the area was going to be rented. We jumped on that and connected with the owner before he put it on the market. We got it! We were lucky and I was relieved.

Chapter 30

INNER HEALING

Did I say that digging into the questions of one's family's toxic patterns was an easy process? Because if I did, I lied. I lied to myself, most definitely. I read two differing opinions on the subject: One, just deal with the here and now with talk therapy. Two, start on the surface to address the symptoms attached to the roots. Roots are your family. I wanted the first option. Because that meant I could potentially change things if they were within my control. Control issues? I laugh in the face of control issues. If the second option was the only cure, it would mean there were more issues below the surface — things I couldn't change. Or so I thought. The problem arose when I realized I would not be able to control a single thing if I didn't know what, or who, was behind the curtain!

There is a tension in going down the second road. The human mind has been conditioned, programmed, and set to think and believe certain things. This conditioning can be implied or spoken, or it can come from what wasn't spoken. It can come from what was shown by act or omission. The tension is in trying to break free from this mind-set. The brain will most assuredly try to convince you that you are crazy. Mine had and was. With this route, people may even exhibit symptoms of bipolar disorder (I am raising my hand) or manic or depressive episodes. It is because a system within is being unearthed. A narrative that was laid in the neurons of the brain is being challenged.

It was essential I continue in order to disrupt neuropathways in my brain that no longer suited me. During this season of inner healing, I was not only struggling on the inside with what I was discovering about myself and my family, I was also being challenged on the outside by my family and friends. Note: Going with the flow will feel different from going against it. In this search I had to ask myself if it was worth it. Could I just go with the flow? The answer for me was no. I could not. I would not. I will not eat green eggs and ham.

With my unearthing came more drinking, as if I wasn't drinking enough already. I had to quiet down the voices and numb myself. Drinking was the most socially acceptable answer to that for my lifestyle. Drinking was fine with me, until it wasn't anymore. When I realized I desired to be more present with Livvy and that drinking was my pattern of shutting down, I tried to slow down the drinking. It was then I realized I couldn't.

I chatted a little bit about this struggle with both Aaron and my inner healing pastor. But I didn't unveil the entire truth. Shame number one — I was hiding. I kept thinking I could get it under control without making a big deal about it. Aaron referred me to Life Skills International in the spring of 2017. It was a weekly, three-hour class for thirty-five weeks with ten other ladies. Aaron figured the group support would be a good segue to my meeting one-on-one with him.

Life Skills material covered issues from in utero to adulthood and healthy adult relationships. The course expounded on unhealthy and healthy patterns and the skills needed to create healthy ones. That all sounded great, and I needed more support for my journey anyway. The major issue was childcare for Livvy and my having to drive ninety minutes to class every week. When my sister and mom agreed to help when Vince wasn't able to be home for Livvy, I made the commitment to drive every week to class — uphill both ways, in the snow (totally kidding, but it sure felt like it).

In Life Skills, I felt like I was being blasted by a fire hydrant with information that was blowing my mind. Life Skills was compounding the work I was doing with the inner healing pastor. I was learning (or unlearning) lifetimes of toxic patterns. It was in this class that I discovered two amazing books that forever changed me and I still reference. If I come across either in a used bookstore, I take it home with me. Those books are John Bradshaw's Healing the Shame that Binds You and Melody Beattie's Codependent No More. I cried through most of both of them. In reading Codependent No More, I realized the depth of alcoholism in my family. I felt deeply for my mom for having an alcoholic father and how it impacted her parenting me. I also realized how the alcoholic consumption of my own fathers — both the father who raised me, and the father who left me — affected me.

My mom's father lost his life in the bottle. He died alone and wasn't found until a few days later. He lived a sad life. In discussing these sorrows with Vince, I found out that Vince's grandfather also died in a bottle, angry and detached from the family. Vince and I considered these scenarios and began looking at them in relation to our own. It wasn't long after I read these books and was well into Life Skills that I decided to stop drinking. But I didn't realize how much I needed to drink. I would do well, then slip back into the need again. I wasn't sharing my struggle with anyone. I was ashamed and gripped by my need to drink, and I did not want to alarm anyone, thinking it wasn't an issue for anyone except myself. It worried me, though, that it would soon start shaping Livvy.

Did I mention that digging into the questions of your family's toxic patterns was an easy process? I lied. I lied to myself, most definitely. Choosing the second path is not for the faint of heart. Or maybe if you are faint of heart, you will need the second path to get to the heart of the matter.

Chapter 31

LIFE SKILLS

Around the time I was heavily processing family roots in my Life Skills class, my inner healing work with the retired pastor was coming to an end. She had sat with me for months while I dug up family information. I had interviewed a lot of family members, and some more than once. Each person had their version of the family story, and by asking them similar questions, I could see a bigger, clearer picture than the single side I had formerly known. Pastor Clarke recognized I had done a lot of heavy lifting to identify some intense family patterns and suggested she bring in reinforcement to complete my time with her. I agreed and she brought in her former partner.

We sat across from one another in her living room, the two retired women on one side, me on the other. It was time for me to share my deepest, darkest fears so they could walk me into freedom through inner healing. I shared my struggle with alcohol, the fear around my molestation and the shadowy figure related to it. I shared about the disconnect during intimacy and some of the things I heard in my head during sex, including, but not limited to, what I had learned about

Aunt Alpha's rape and being trafficked by her father. I cried. I wailed through the sharing in complete shame and terror, as though the demons in my past, in my family's past, were haunting me, not wanting me to share, not wanting me to bring the darkness into the light. I cried so hard that in some moments, I was gasping for air.

The two women sat in compassion. I expected some reaction, an expression of disgust or shock. I expected to receive what I had offered myself for so many years — judgment. They neither reacted nor offered shame. Instead, they had expressions of compassion and understanding on their faces, as though they had heard what I was saying before. After I completed sharing my deepest darks, all my terror, disgusting images, and the perverted voices I had heard in my head, they both smiled. I was on the path to healing. It was a huge purge, and I hadn't expected that just in the telling, I would feel lighter. But I did.

After I was done, they gave me some prayers they had written for me to read aloud. Then they asked me to close my eyes and imagine being in a place of pure light. They invited Jesus into the space, and I began to sense immense light and love and freedom overwhelming me in all my dark places. The overarching feeling was acceptance. It was like the light overtook the dark in all those stories and places where darkness had been a bully.

The greatest good that came from the inner healing was my no longer feeling terror from my unsaid struggles. I had been terrified to even mention to anyone else the terrors I suffered alone, and I had been terrified to hear stories about someone else being molested, or beaten, or raped, or trafficked. I was scared of being sucked into my own darkness if anyone dared share their own. The strange thing was, I had a deep desire to help people in dark places. But I could never go too far into the darkness with anyone because it terrified me. If someone was telling a story, or even if I was reading something associated with abuse (like The Sexual Healing Journey), I would have to terminate the conversation or walk away or stop reading. I couldn't handle it. Movies were the worst. I can't tell you how many times I had night terrors from watching a movie that suddenly had a rape scene or abuse was implied. But now I was beginning to sense a greater level of mobility in my being.

I wish I could say this handled it all and life never had another struggle for me. But that wouldn't be true. What did happen was that a few more layers of the onion were being peeled away. I was getting closer to the core of whatever was festering below the surface. There was so much I still didn't know or understand. But in that moment, for these two precious retired inner healing women, I was so grateful. They started something very deep inside me. There would be no turning back, not permanently anyway.

Chapter 32

INHERITED FAMILY TRAUMA

Life Skills was all-consuming, and it seemed I was noticing toxic patterns everywhere. It took a lot of willpower not to become a judgmental critic. The patterns I was seeing did, however, stir a desire in me to change the way I was parenting Livvy.

The main pattern I wanted to correct was reacting from fear -- fear of the shadowy figure and just fear itself. A close second was the pattern of codependency passed down from my family. There was so much to learn, and I wanted Vince to learn it, too. It wouldn't be effective for me to teach him all I was learning; that was for me. But I wanted him to look below the surface, too, and see why he acted the way he did.

About halfway through Life Skills, there was a homework assignment. We had to draft a personal timeline, or diagram, showing in chronological order the significant events in our lives, such as family life, education, career, relationships, marriage, and then where on that line we experienced such things as highs, lows, abuse, drugs, alcohol, abandonment, or neglect. It was one of the few assignments that we had to present to the entire class. Talk about mortifying. This was a very difficult assignment but less difficult since having told my story in inner healing. The assignment put my life into a new perspective on how my past, my family, and my upbringing had affected my choices and relationships. It was a concise overview. After each person presented their timeline (almost always crying through most of it), the class was free to ask questions. The idea was that the people listening might connect some dots to help illuminate their own patterns.

Some of my patterns surprised me, but a lot had already been illuminated in the inner healing work I had been doing. This project helped me see more about how my fears were connected to my roots. As I dug deeper, I stumbled upon a book called It Didn't Start with You: How Inherited Family Trauma Shapes Who We Are and How to End the Cycle by Mark Wolynn. This was the linchpin! It spoke to the family patterns and what I had read about online about cognitive resonance. This book called my experience related to Aunt Alpha an inherited memory. I had somehow inherited Aunt Alpha's trauma. What I loved most about this book, other than the cathartic release and connection to my experience, was that the author provided exercises on how to heal through and release the trauma stored in our memory from our ancestors. Wow! This was life-changing. This was fuel for my soul.

Regarding the codependent pattern with Livvy, I was just learning what it meant to be codependent. We toss that word around a lot in society, and there is more than one way it manifests. Typically, most of us fall into one of the four codependent patterns. I noticed it when Livvy began asking me if I was angry with her and following that with "What can I do to make Mommy feel better?" Light bulb. It is not a child's job to make a parent feel better, or anyone for that matter. No one can change someone's feelings. This statement needs repeating. No one can change someone else's feelings. Humans are not that powerful. Someone can impact your feelings, but you make the choice to feel something based on past experiences and your understanding of events that are about you and your story.

In this epiphany about Livvy trying to fix me, I was dead set against furthering the pattern. I had to get really serious about how I used my emotions to control people. I was being passive and expecting others to change how they acted to make me feel better. If I wanted Livvy to leave me alone because I needed down time, I would act out emotionally, and she would retreat or be extra sweet and walk on eggshells for my emotional health. She was changing who she was to be who I needed her to be. Sound familiar? This is the same pattern I grew up with. This is the same pattern my parents grew up with. Dare I say it was a longstanding pattern? It was a pattern I was ready to do battle with for the health of Livvy and myself. I wanted to build a relationship with her in which she could be herself, in which any feelings or thoughts she had were for her and not for me.

I decided I wanted relationships in which I could create a space for healthy communication about feelings, to be able to observe them without needing to react, a space where I could appropriately ask for what I needed or wanted and allow the other person to say yes or no to my request. This was the healthy type of relationship I was searching for with Livvy, with Vince, with myself.

It wasn't until I began unwinding this pattern and how it looked that Vince agreed we both struggled with codependency. He thought it was a pattern just in my family based on the one-dimensional definition most of us have come to know. It wasn't until I pointed it out in him one evening while he was lashing out at Livvy that he agreed to sign up for Life Skills himself. He was trying to exit to the back patio, and Livvy was playing by the shutter doors. She opened one as he was walking by. It jammed his toe and he yelled at her.

"Livvy, you hurt me!" he screamed.

She backed away in shame, not even sure exactly what she had done.

"What happened? Why are you angry?" she asked.

"You hurt me and made me angry, Livvy!" he barked.

Pretty typical, right? Well, that's codependency.

Immediately I reacted. "She didn't make you anything! You got hurt and you got angry," I snapped.

After he calmed down, I explained to him how Life Skills could help him with his reactive behavior (and mine too) of accusing anyone of controlling his emotions. I gave him this example of what I was learning:

Livvy wasn't responsible for him stubbing his toe. She wasn't responsible for his pain or his reaction to his pain. She most definitely didn't make him angry. He apologized to Livvy and explained that she couldn't control his feelings and he was sorry for accusing her of hurting him and making him angry. Repair made.

He signed up for Life Skills.

Chapter 33

PROGRESS

Although I loved Mark Wolynn's book, it began to stir something in me that felt like anger. It was directed toward God. Why was I handed this bag of shit for genes? Why wasn't God fixing me? Hadn't I served Him well enough, long enough? Resentment was churning, festering. The result was I was distancing myself from asking the spiritual questions, or more truthfully, I was distancing myself from myself. Instead of having my quiet prayer and meditation time in the mornings, I would sleep. Then when I awoke, I felt shame. The day would start, and I would be behind.

Acknowledging the progress I had made and felt with the inner healing wasn't helping. Not only was it not helping, it was hindering my progress. I argued that I had done enough, and why wasn't my life changing and at my pace, meaning, quickly? My fear began to intensify, not lessen. I needed to fall asleep with the lights on. I came into the house feeling I was being watched and checked each room, closet, and shower to make sure no one was there. Fear felt gripping and all-encompassing. If Vince had an away gig, some nights I would not be able to sleep at all. Some nights I would lie there frozen in my own fear, not daring to move. Other nights I would get up and play the song by Hillsong United "Not Today" with the line "Let the devil know not today" — on repeat — and pray through the night. It was all I knew to do.

As hard as I was trying, my life felt disconnected again. I hadn't known at the time what a huge pile of shit I had to work through. The process is much like peeling back the layers of an onion. And when there are several onions, there are a lot of layers to go through. Thinking I could do just one healing modality, for a few months, and be cured of a lifetime, or multiple lifetimes, of trauma, I was kidding myself. But I didn't know that then, so I felt despondent.

Where had this started? What was under it all? Every time I asked these questions of myself, or God, I would sense a finger pointing back into the darkness of time. The Life Skills homework and Mark Wolynn's book pushed me to delve even deeper into my family tree. Since my Life Skills class talked about making a genogram, I looked up more details on how that may help me. A genogram is a pictorial display of a person's family relationships but goes deeper by looking at patterns.

My sister had just introduced me to an author named Brené Brown. I became hooked on her work and began reading through all her published books: Rising Strong; Braving the Wilderness; The Gifts of Imperfection; Daring Greatly; The Power of Vulnerability; Men, Women and Worthiness; and I Thought It Was Just Me, But It Wasn't. If you aren't familiar with her work, she is a shame researcher. I cried through most of her books. In Braving the Wilderness, she talked about making a genogram for herself. She said her genogram had illuminated patterns she didn't want to carry on. It was so impactful, she said, that it led her to quit drinking and smoking. Maybe facing the family stuff would influence me for the better, too?

I went over to my Nana's house and sat in the living room. It doesn't take much to get grandparents to tell stories. I think they live for it. Literally. I thought by now she would be tired of telling them to me or answering my questions. But she never got tired of it. There were ancestors in the family tree on my Ancestry.com account that had interesting data. I wanted to know more. Pressing in I gently asked her about her own mother and father. It didn't take much to get her rolling with the stories. I took notes and tried to connect her interpretation to what I had been researching on my family tree. Who were these people? What kind of life had they lived? What had motivated them? What burdens had they carried?

Nana told me her mother left the family one day after she had a fit of rage. Nana explained that her mom, Jewel, just popped one day and started beating Nana's little brother with a whip. Nana and her older sister had to pull their mother off their brother. Nana attributed it to hormones and later in life figured her mom had a bad bout with menopause. I suspected more. Nonetheless, her mother abandoned them, leaving Nana and her older sister to find a husband at fourteen and fifteen years old.

So, what was so dark in Nana's mother's life that was her burden? Just menopause? I wasn't convinced. Jewel went on to marry three more times — that we are aware of. What was her struggle? I asked Nana to tell me about Jewel's parents, Nana's grandparents. What had happened in Jewel's childhood that may have impacted her parenting, or lack thereof? What possesses a parent to leave their children? Knowing some of my biological father's story made me reflect that there was more to Jewel's story, too.

Nana had nothing but good things to say about her grandparents. They had even lived with her for a short time when she was young. Something wasn't adding up. But then I remembered that her grandmother had been divorced early in life. So I asked Nana about that divorce. I hit the gold mine. Her biological grandfather wasn't allowed to come around. He was a bad man. Oscar Richard Jones, or O.R., as she called him. Nana's grandma fled, leaving three little kids behind with O.R. because he was abusive. My jaw dropped!

"She left her kiddos with an abusive man?" I asked.

"I guess so. I never thought much about that," Nana replied.

Her grandma, Lottie Pearl, fled for her life but couldn't take the kids. The kids were left with an abusive father, my ancestor. Lottie Pearl remarried right away and had another family. No doubt the kids left behind in the first marriage didn't fare well, one being my great-grandma Jewel. I asked what happened to Jewel, being raised by O.R. Jones. Nana said that Jewel was always a favorite, as she understood it, but that Jewel's sister, Aunt Helen, was raped by her father. She was damaged and never could have kids. Nana described her as lovely and funny, and Helen always wished to adopt Nana because her sister Jewel already had so many kids. Nana explained that Aunt Helen had been a lady of the night. She drank a lot and smoked nonstop. I could tell my Nana cared for her very much. I asked about the third child.

"Casey Jones. My favorite uncle. He left me his Bible. I still have it," Nana said.

"Why was he your favorite?" I asked.

Casey lived on a train (I often wonder now if he was the Casey Jones Johnny Cash wrote about). Casey ran away from home when he was young because his father would beat him. Casey resolved to be a hobo, returning home every now and then to see his mother. He would visit Jewel, his sister, when Nana was young. I could see in her eyes how much she deeply cared for him as well. I was beginning to see Nana's depth of compassion for what she hadn't even consciously pieced together — a life of pain for our family. A legacy of brokenness. The story goes that Casey went on to kill a man in self-defense, living life as a runaway fugitive until his demise — suicide on a train. He left a note and all the money in his wallet to his sister Jewel.

I have a few photos of O.R. Jones. He looked smooth, with a suit and flashy car. I am not sure what he did for a living, but I know what he did to our family. He went on to take his young niece as his wife, and after the kids were grown, he seems to have disappeared from their life, or they disappeared from his.

Chapter 34

BUSINESS COACH

The news about Nana's family caused notable sorrow for me. It all struck a chord. But it didn't seem to have fazed her. Had she already processed it, or had she never pieced the pain together?

It was late spring of 2017 and I was becoming increasingly unhappy with my career, maybe because of the sorrow of my family legacy, maybe because of what I was learning in Life Skills. I was told the more I unearthed, the more the soul would feel like a tilled field. That was true, I guess.

It had not been even two years since we started our new business. But it had become all-consuming, and I was starting to resent my partners. The three of us owners decided to hire a business coach because Matt's wife was transitioning into the business full time. The business was growing fast, and we had pulled back the reins on taking new clients so we could improve our systems. Since we needed more hands-on-deck, Matt's wife was the best choice, since she was a vested partner.

The coach met with us corporately, and then each of us one-on-one. It was during my one-on-one that he inquired on my "why." Why was I doing this job? Did I like it and why or why not? On and on. The questions felt like classical homeopathy all over again. After our meeting, he closed his notebook and looked at me.

"You don't need to be doing this job. I recommend you quit. It's not your passion," he stated.

My jaw dropped. I could not disagree. But I had just built this company and was practically killing myself to keep it growing, training my partners in real estate, and I had given up a constant paycheck when I left my previous job. This was my investment!

His conclusion was that if I stayed in a position I didn't like, where I didn't see a future, and that I was beginning to resent, I would destroy the success of the company and my relationships with my partners. From the outside, I guess that was true. It just wasn't something I could fathom — quitting again?

On my drive home I contemplated possibilities. None made practical or rational sense. What could I do? How could I earn an income with something I enjoyed? I knew well enough that I was liking my independence from a boss. So maybe I just work for myself? That sounded very intimidating. This wasn't selling cookies or bracelets like when I was a kid. It wasn't mowing lawns or babysitting for spending money. This was my livelihood. I had a kid now. These, no doubt, are all the reasons people stay in a dead-end job that leaves them feeling numb and passionless. The point was, I didn't trust myself to be on my own.

Maybe I could pray about it, and God would give me the answer? Maybe Vince could tell me what to do? Maybe I could call Cathy? Who can tell me what to do?

This train of thought shocked me. I was looking for someone else to tell me what was best for me. Tell Bethany what to do, what to be. Tell Bethany how high, and she will jump higher. I squirmed with the idea of choosing something on my own. My old patterns of being who others needed me to be was surfacing again, in my career.

I did talk to Vince about it. But he was all for me picking what I believed was best for me. I did pray about it. But God was essentially silent on the topic. I resented Him for his lack of encouragement. Maybe I could ask for a sign? Would that work? I surely wasn't hearing anything else in my heart or from God! So, I did. I asked that if I was meant to go out on my own that I would get a call to list a house for sale. It was almost an impossible request, and maybe I was setting too high of a target for my sign.

The most important thing was deciding for myself. The coach was right. My attitude and indifference would put a damper on the growth of the company. My partners had to know how I felt. I had to tell Matt, and soon before I lost courage and fell back into status quo.

Matt didn't take the news well. It would mean that if he didn't get his broker's license, the business would need to close down, or find a new broker. Both options would toss a wrench into the growth plans for the business. But I stood firm. I wanted to buy out my portion of the business. What I would do next, I wasn't sure. But I told them I would branch off and do real estate sales on my own. I agreed that I wouldn't practice property management or be in competition with them (I kept doing that to ease the transition). I would even help Matt by sponsoring him to become a broker. Was he ready? Did he even want that? Probably not, but he realized that was the best plan if I was indeed leaving them.

Matt's wife was supportive and diplomatic, just like my former boss's wife was. However, I felt the tension, as she knew I held the business knowledge for the team. I respect the fact that she prioritized our relationship over her worry for the company. Matt did, too, in some respects, but his frustration was more noticeable. Matt would try to not be resentful. I can't blame him for how he handled it, and there were a few moments in the months of transition where he could have behaved differently. But, in hindsight, I had chosen it. As an active participant in the making of the business, I had chosen the whole thing for myself — being submissive and allowing another man to take the reins in my life. That was all my doing. I had to own that. Matt was just being himself.

Agreeing to consult as broker of record until Matt got his broker's license would keep me with the business until November 2017. We met with attorneys and tax consultants and ultimately a business appraiser to negotiate a buyout amount. At the end of the day, I settled for what it cost me to go without a paycheck the first year of business (ultimately that was taken from me by the IRS in taxes due — yay). I was moving away from relationships I attracted based on my need to be needed.

About my sign. I got it. I asked for a call from someone to sell their house. It would be my first sale on my very own. One day after I made the decision to go out on my own, I got that call while I was showing a rental property. It was an old friend, three times removed. Their son had referred me and wanted me to list their million-dollar home for sale. Tears rolled down my face as I listened to her message.

I was learning what it felt like to trust myself.

I was growing.

Chapter 35

MY SIGN

You would think when someone gets a sign that is far-fetched and seems to come from out of the blue, like the call I got to list the house, it would inspire faith. Maybe I was just ungrateful or forgetful. For a little while, I was happy, but as the house sat and sat and sat — open house after open house, July passed, August passed, September passed — I was beginning to feel hopeless. I started to question my "sign."

To be honest, my faith was already struggling, and the house not selling just reinforced the struggle. My time with Matt and his wife in the business was coming to an end. My paycheck would fully depend on my success out on my own. I was bouncing back and forth between searching for my Heavenly Father and deciding He was distant. The second thought resonated the strongest. Maybe God the Father was like my earthly fathers.

We were closing in on Matt getting his broker's license and me exiting the company. I had decided if I sold the million-dollar house, Vince and Livvy and I would take a trip to Europe for Christmas. We had always talked about going to Italy or France. The trip started looking impossible. Instead, I planned for Livvy and me to travel to see Cathy in Illinois. Cathy was my safe haven. It felt like home when I went to her house. She had been my mentor and friend since before I met Vince. With my struggling faith, I knew that was where I needed to go. My birthday was coming up, so I booked some plane tickets for a week in December.

Amidst all this work crap and questioning my faith, I was also closing in on my Life Skills graduation. I felt confident enough to have another serious talk with my mom. There were things that had happened between us that caused me to pull away from her, and I wasn't sure how to address them. Inside I was a scared little girl. How could I own my truth and share my heart without the childhood fear? I wasn't sure, but I knew I had to talk to her afraid or not.

My mom and I had struggled in our relationship after I had met my biological father when I was eighteen. The relationship got worse when I got engaged at nineteen and crumbled when I moved to Australia after I got married. Maybe we had always struggled. I just didn't know because I was a kid. How was I to know the difference? The amazing thing about kids, they need their parents for survival. We ally with our parents when we are young regardless of the circumstances.

I had connected with my mom at different times during my darkness, my questioning it, and the therapy modalities I had gone through. She and my dad had allowed us to live with them during my mold poisoning, when the darkness had taken over my mind. She wanted a relationship with me; I wanted one with her. We just kept smacking up against each other somehow, and then we each retreated to our corners. I know now we were making progress. Somehow it never felt like enough.

I prepared my notes and called my mom for the talk. I was so nervous. I felt like I was committing relational suicide. I imagined she would react and storm off and we would be back to ground zero. We had this pattern. But I wanted it different. I wanted to lean into my mom and not pull away, to bond and not feel distant.

How horribly I did with this conversation! I laid out some basic requests, my version of boundaries. However, I had only just started to learn about healthy boundaries, and I wasn't quite sure how to implement them. Instead of putting up healthy boundaries, I ended up telling her what to do and what not to do. Major fail. She sat across from me in my home office and cried in frustration. I walled-up and went into protection mode. Growing up I had always sensed she used her emotions as manipulation. Maybe she didn't do it knowingly, but it affected me. Emotional manipulation shook me at my core.

Running away was my first reaction. If I couldn't say no, stand my ground, and own my truth because I was shakin' in my boots, then I should run away and avoid the situation at all costs. I did this for years, all the while pretending I was the boss. My "runaway" didn't look timid or fearful or intimidated. My "runaway" was feeling calloused and shut down, pushing people away, some may even say stoic. It reminded me of the day my dad disowned me prior to my wedding. I knew what I had to do to protect myself — be on the outside who and what they needed me to be, shut down on the inside behind a shield of steel.

This interaction with my mom went badly, but I am happy to report it was the start of my having the courage to face the real issues behind my pain. Even though she was crying and upset, I didn't run away. I took Mark Wolynn's advice and stayed in the game because I wanted to lean in. Even if I couldn't quite find my way yet, I was taking my first steps.

Even though I was questioning my "sign," I worked hard to get my client's house sold. It seemed to take forever, and there were enough ups and downs to make me nauseous from the roller coaster ride. But in November 2017, when my contract with Matt and his wife ended, the house sold! I was so proud of myself! We were able to book those tickets to Europe for three weeks over our Christmas and New Year break, but first, Livvy and I were going to see Cathy the first week of December. My year that had started off so badly at the red house was ending on an up note.

Chapter 36

SOUL CARE

Visiting Cathy always nourished my soul. It had been over three years since I had been to see her, and a lot had transpired since then. Our visits consisted of long conversations that went on for days.

It wasn't that we hadn't talked between visits, we just weren't much for phone conversations very often. She had the highlights, but not the details. I was catching her up on the inner healing work, Life Skills, mold poisoning, grief processing over David's passing, marriage, pregnancy and parenting, the darkness, and therapy. She was most interested in the inner healing work because she had recently gone through a similar process called Soul Care. She mentioned her Soul Care work had ended with a process called deliverance. I knew that word. The church I grew up in practiced what they called deliverances, which were similar to Catholic exorcisms. Watching them was terrifying. They were not kind or effective. Because of witnessing them, I ran away from anything that reminded me of exorcisms.

Cathy and I were typically magnetized toward deep conversations, so we always seemed to return to the topic of inner healing and deliverance. Cathy asked if, during my inner healing, the retired pastor had "cast anything out." That's how she put it. I couldn't recall that happening.

Cathy got a familiar look on her face — thinking, questioning. I knew there was more behind it.

"Hmm," she said with her thinking face.

"Tell me what you're thinking," I said.

"It's just that I understand that if you don't actually cast anything out, then was it comprehensive?" she wondered.

Neither of us had the answer, but we wanted to know. Her experience with Soul Care and my experience with inner healing mimicked each other in a lot of ways. Hers ended with "casting out" and mine didn't. What did it mean? She asked if she could order me the book Soul Care.

"It is like gold!" she said.

"How could I say no? Order it for me." It would be my birthday gift.

It came the next day, but I saved it for my trip to Europe.

Once again spending time with Cathy was nourishing for my soul, and the timing was perfect. And she got to spend time with my Livvy. The trip was greatly needed and well worth it.

Two weeks later, Vince and Livvy and I boarded the train to downtown San Diego, where we would stay overnight and then hop on our early-morning Christmas flight to London. I was so excited. It felt like a trip of a lifetime. We would start in London, fly to Venice, and end in Paris. We found some amazing vacation rentals and would stay at each place for about five days, all courtesy of my commission from selling my client's house.

Christmas morning, I stuffed the Soul Care book in my carry-on to read on the plane until I fell asleep. We got settled into our massive airplane and had some food, and then while Vince and Livvy agreed on a movie, I grabbed my book. I've read books before, lots of them. I have favorites. But this book sucked me in like nothing I had read before. It was something supernatural. My heart pounded, but not in fear, in expectation. This book had practical advice, real life stories, and answers to the problems I had been facing. In hindsight, maybe it wasn't a book for a twelve-hour plane ride because my eyes bubbled over with tears. I couldn't hold back the pain I felt reading the stories and how they were so connected to my current life predicament.

Chapter after chapter I was captivated. I fell asleep, but only because I couldn't read anymore from my tear-glazed eyes. Once we arrived in London, I was reading every free moment. This wasn't a book you could gloss over. It was not just a reading book, it was also an activity book. I delved into each chapter like it held a key. Chapters on identity, family patterns, wounds, fears, and then forgiveness and repentance. Each one was chock-full of sustenance.

I could go on to tell you about London and Italy and Paris, and they were amazing. But the trip's silver lining for me was Soul Care, a book I could have read anywhere, but I happened to read it on our dream trip.

When we landed in London, I had bouts of dizziness that didn't end until Italy, where I connected the dizziness to a resentment I was holding toward my brother-in-law. When I realized this connection and made the committed to release the resentment, the dizziness vanished. When we got to Italy, I was constipated. It wasn't until Paris that I began to connect so many of my fears to holding back and holding in, hence constipation. Paris was probably the best part of the trip because I wasn't backed up or dizzy. What was this book doing to me?

Paris was also the place where I finished the book while Vince and Livvy were out on an adventure. Looking out the window over the city from our second-story vacation rental, I sat and sobbed. The author, Dr. Rob Reimer, finished the book with a chapter on deliverance. He shared twenty years of experiential detail with story after story of people who inherited demons from their generational line. It didn't sound possible — born with demons? But I was living proof. His stories resonated with me at such a high frequency, I could not deny what I was reading. But what could be done about it?

I had to call Cathy when I got back to the States. I was sure she already knew much about what I discovered. I had demons. She told me about a place in Florida that could help us learn more about this subject and possibly get rid of my darkness at a level the inner healing and the myriad of other modalities hadn't quite done. We both signed up for the Florida seminar scheduled for May 2018.

If my faith had been shaky before, now it was on the verge of dissipating altogether. I was questioning God on His design to allow people to be born with demons from their ancestors' shit. I had been born with a flippin' legacy of brokenness. Facts in place. I couldn't deny the idea about demons because I had all the symptoms. But I was coming to terms with the fact that, if God indeed allowed this, He wasn't a God I wanted to follow.

Chapter 37

DEMONS

The thought of demons wasn't relenting. I sensed that something demonic was attached to my darkness, to my family history of abuse of women, and to my strange connection with Aunt Alpha. My desire to pursue the truth of my family story caused me to think back on things said by different family members about my paternity. Was the man I met actually my biological father? Or was there someone else out there who made me? I had occasionally felt a disconnect on my few visits with him. Was it because I had walls up? Or because I was afraid to get attached because he wasn't the real one? I needed to know for sure. But how?

Questioning my identity had not been an easy path. Could I have just left it well enough alone? Maybe. But I was becoming a truth seeker, and I wanted to know about my true legacy — no doubts. It felt important for me to know my family's truth -- good, bad, and ugly -- for my own healing and to help Livvy know where she came from, too.

Ever since I was young, I had struggled with a sense of worthlessness, being discarded, without value. I had done all I could to outperform, perfect, and push my own limits. I used to think it was to get my parents' love and attention or maybe to capture God's acceptance or approval. Or maybe to capture my own attention, to find love for myself despite how damaged or discarded I felt in my core.

Nonetheless, the desire for this unconditional love, to banish the darkness, to live full-heartedly, and to be whole was my driving force. I heard that children often take traumatic events and project them onto themselves as their own fault. The example I heard was if parents get divorced or a loved one passes, the child automatically thinks, "This is my fault." That idea resonated with me. If my story was so shameful to my parents that they had to cover it up and make a new one, then I must be bad. I felt like something was faulty in me. I didn't see myself as being loved for my true identity. How could I love myself if I didn't see myself as being loved by others for who I was? Abandoned. Was there something I could do to heal the brokenness somehow? I was making some progress, but nothing substantial.

I walked deeper into my wilderness, inspired by reading Brené Brown's Braving the Wilderness. In March 2018 I contacted my biological father and asked if he would do a DNA test with me. My question may have broken his heart, but I needed to end my doubts once and for all. He agreed.

I asked my mom to help with Livvy while I traveled to Fresno to do the DNA test. She was livid! Not about helping with Livvy, but about how I would dare question her! I didn't know at the time the DNA test would offend her. I thought it would bother only my biological father. I see now how she felt my doubt was implicating her as a liar. But there was quite a bit of our story hidden in the dark intentionally or unintentionally. Could someone blame me for wanting to know? Yes. Yes, they could — and they did.

I drove halfway to Fresno and stopped at a vacation rental. I would stay alone. It was nerve-racking, but it had to be done — follow the bunny trail. Maybe it was just who I was — a seeker. Being alone may not seem like a big deal to you, but for someone who had a shadowy dark figure following her and who had to sleep with lights on, it was incredibly frightening. I was doing my best to put on my big girl underwear. But I was terrified. The sky was dark and gloomy. I photographed it for symbolic reasons. I got sick to my stomach and vomited violently that night. It might have been bad salmon — or what I was about to do the next day.

I had scheduled a lunch with my biological father and met him with the Labcorp test kit. We each had to spit into a vial and send them back in a prepackaged box. He was kind, but I could see his uncertainty. I sensed he loved me but didn't know how to show it, or how to be vulnerable. But sorrow would come if I wasn't his after all — for him and for me. It would also leave me with a new search and more strands in the wad of yarn.

We embraced after lunch, and I struck out on my journey back to San Diego. The sun was shining through the clouds with rays of light that had an air of hope. It was completely opposite from my drive up with dark clouds lurking around like a thunderstorm was coming. I snapped another photo of the sky and took a deep breath.

We waited.

April 17, 2018, I got the envelope from Labcorp. Conclusive results — 99.9999% paternity match. I emailed my biological father: "Results are in! You have a baby girl!" He replied: "Baby girl, welcome to the family!! I love you!! Papasan." I sobbed. What a relief to know, yet so much pain was reinforced. The truth often hurts.

Time would only tell if my mom would be okay with my search. That was her journey. Livvy would be turning four in May, and I wanted to invite my biological father to stay with us for her birthday party. It would be the first time he was around my family since 2012. But this time was different.

During his visit this time, my mom wanted the three of us to have a talk together. It had been years since she had spoken to him. I agreed to a short meeting on my back patio, where it felt more neutral and within my control. You guys, this was the first time in my entire life my biological parents sat down with me, the first time the three of us had ever been together. The first time. Maybe the last. I was so overcome with emotion. I was struggling to stay present. It felt strange and scary at the same time. They were both expressing concern regarding my search and how it was affecting my health. Undoubtedly, I hadn't kept that a secret. My mom turned reactive and heated within seconds, and Vince took Livvy inside.

I honestly can't recall what was said. Something about my questioning her truthfulness about the paternity, her faithfulness during their marriage, and about my search and how it was affecting me and the family. It was all very blurry. There were things between them I hadn't understood at the time. I just know I felt threatened. My biological father was very quiet. As I understand it, that was his nature. It wasn't too long before he noticed my tears and my feeling overwhelmed. He asked my mom to leave. We had hit some wall. I wish I had been more present. I wish I had felt safer, that I had been more whole and grown.

I wish.

Chapter 38

ZOMBIES

Since I had always wanted to go to grad school, and it was part of my plan with the Life Coach Experience, I figured I would look into a program in Florida when I attended the seminar there with Cathy in May. It was a master's program for Christian Counseling. I wasn't sure I was quite buying into Christianity at this point, but it was the faith I had always followed and wasn't publicly denying anything just yet. So I made an appointment to meet with the dean of admissions during my trip.

I arrived a day before Cathy and had my own hotel room. Another night alone I wasn't looking forward to. I decided I would start on some notes about the demonic darkness I had felt and maybe connect my current drinking struggle with my desire to numb. While journaling in the hotel, I had all the lights on. I was terrified of being visited by the shadowy figure.

My scribbles drifted toward my heartbreak over my breakup with David. I had shut myself in at my parents' place and spent months on my knees praying David would come back to me. I thought that If I could fix our marriage, then I could fix being rejected and abandoned once and for all. Sad to see now that it wasn't even David that I really wanted. It was to fix my little broken, abandoned heart. I wanted my father's love.

The first guy I dated after David was a guy named Geoff, and I believed I loved him. It was unrequited love and more heartbreak. He only ever wanted me when he had too much to drink. Pattern? After my heartbreak with Geoff, and still confused about whom I loved more, David or Geoff, I met Colt. I am not sure choosing Colt was a conscious decision, but I see now how my story with him played into the hand that made the most sense to me at the time — I felt used and worthless.

Colt was a Taylor Swift song, or several Taylor Swift songs. I knew he was trouble when he walked in. Loving him was red. He was handsome, cunning, funny, and trouble all the way. I was ready to say yes to trouble. None of my friends liked him. None of his friends liked him.

Colt was a liar and spun a lot of yarn. I knew he was a liar, and I listened to him as if I didn't care. If he thought I bought his lies, he was stupider than I imagined. The more we hung out, the meaner he got until he eventually took to physically and verbally hurting me. Sadly, I had issues, too. Being pushed around caused me to feel something. It had to hurt to get through my callous surface. It was distressing and alluring. I see how this can be a reason for some women to stay with men like this. To feel something. Passion is what I was looking for, and passion is what I got. In all the wrong ways.

But I was still human, and even though I knew better, my heart got attached to being with someone. To being touched and desired, even if just carnally. It was a slippery slope. One evening on our drive home from dinner, I was driving, and he tried to grab the steering wheel, making the car swerve. I smacked his hand away. I was fuming inside. Was he trying to kill us? That was the last straw. I took him home. I didn't get out. I didn't say goodbye. It was over. I couldn't fix him or myself. I was beginning to see how my choice in men was my trying to fix the brokenness inside me. Dare I say, to make my alcoholic daddy love me.

My journal notes on David, Geoff, Colt, and more did show a pattern. I sat in the brightly lit hotel room listening to music, and the song "Zombie" by The Cranberries came on. If you know the song, you know the intensity. The lyrics, "it's in your head", repeat over and over. But it just wasn't in my head, it was also in my family. The abuse was in the relationship patterns, my mother's pattern, her mother's, and on and on for generations back. My heart ached for us, for the brokenness.

I was hoping for a miracle in the next few days at this seminar. Maybe it would shine a light on some solid solutions. It did turn out to be enlightening. I had never before heard anyone talk about people like me living with demons that cause physical ailments, depression and confusion, detachment and numbness. I had experienced all these things. The speaker even talked about family curses and patterns and demons that can be inherited — just like Dr. Rob Reimer had talked about in his Soul Care book.

The last day of the seminar, the facilitators asked only the people who believed they had an issue with demons influencing them, and who wanted prayer, to come back after lunch. I fell into both categories. My church upbringing never taught these types of lessons, so I was happy to hear there might be an answer other than pining away endlessly without hope.

The meeting was different. We sat on chairs scattered throughout the room for privacy, and the facilitators rotated through the room to pray for people. My major memory of the event was feeling ill. I had dizzy spells, and my hearing would wane. My eyes glazed over, much like when I was reading the book The Sexual Healing Journey. I didn't take much from the prayer time, and I wasn't sure it was working. But one prayer did impact me. The facilitator intuitively prayed to break a family curse of alcoholism and commanded, "Spirit of alcoholism, up and out!" If there was one thing I had tried, it was kicking the drinking habit, the need to numb using alcohol. I hoped her prayer would work for me.

That day was May 18, 2018. It's the day I miraculously stopped drinking. I was one step closer to understanding the deep inner connection I had to my family through trauma and shared memories. One step closer to knowing what to do with the darkness. I was excited to share this seminar with Vince, and I had to read Soul Care again. What more could I learn? Something was working.

Chapter 39

THE PROBLEM OF PAIN

Vince was impressed with what I had learned at the seminar, but what I had learned was for me, not him. He was sweet, agreeing it would impact my journey, secretly hoping I would be less numbed out and more connected. We had been, for the most part, independently working out our shit, and there still were times when our issues affected one another. We gave a lot of grace to each other, and it was improving our marriage, and our parenting. Vince was learning quite a bit in Life Skills. It seemed to be triggering a little depression and confusion, though. I made space for that. I had just been through the program myself.

Vince worked the Orange County Fair every summer. He stayed in a hotel a few hours away and would come home when the Fair was closed on Mondays and Tuesdays. Sometimes Livvy and I would go stay with him in the hotel. I still hated staying home without him. It seemed like I could never quite sleep. Something was always lurking around, and I was losing faith quickly. How could someone like me be in dire search for answers, spiritual or natural, and never quite seem to overcome the struggles?

I went to church every once in a while. I didn't really enjoy it, but sometimes I needed the encouragement. One Sunday I just sat and cried through the songs. God felt so distant. I felt a void. My pastor came up and asked how I was doing. I told her I wasn't sure God was real, and if He was, He didn't seem to care about me very much. I expected some religious answer and lack of understanding. Not that she was that way, but it was what I had come to expect from church people. She was the same one who had sat and held my hand while I cried when I found out about Vince's emotional affair. She was soft and kindhearted.

"Life is tough. We aren't promised an easy path, but keep wrestling. God isn't afraid of your doubt. He doesn't mind if you are angry at Him. Sometimes losing your faith is the best way to find the truth," she said.

I wasn't expecting that. I had been hanging on to my faith, but maybe she was right. Maybe what I had come to understand wasn't God at all. Maybe that was why I was faltering. I could let go. I could express my anger. After all, there was a lot pent up.

Livvy and I decided to visit Vince in Orange County. I listened to Bob Goff on a podcast as we drove. I had just read his book, Everybody Always: Becoming Love in a World Full of Setbacks and Difficult People. I was intrigued by his life and wanted to hear more. His podcast was on vows. He was speaking to a law class at Pepperdine University. He cracked a lot of jokes and was very captivating. One thing really spoke to me, and I reflect on it a lot still. He said that when you set out toward a passion, write down your reason. He called it a vow. Why are you passionate about your pursuit? Because when you're in the middle of the pursuit, you will grow weary. There will be trials and struggles. You will want to quit. If you have forgotten why you were passionate at the start, you may just quit. His idea was that most people who quit have forgotten the passion they had at the outset. He said write it down, the why. Make it visceral. And if it isn't, your reason won't get you through to completion.

I contemplated this advice while in Orange County. Did I have a passion? What was my passion? Did I just want to attend grad school for the degree so I could wave it around and be somebody with a PhD? I looked down at Livvy standing in the kitchen, and I saw something I had never seen before. I wanted to understand her. I wanted to know about her development, how humans develop. Why and how. And how our families connect, and what is our spiritual connection. She would be my vow. Her life gave reason and passion to mine.

I had just read the book The Problem of Pain by C.S. Lewis. The book was life-altering. I know I say that about a lot of books, but this one really illuminated free will, humanity, and why we have pain. I had never heard such a topic! I was driving home, alone in the car, and contemplating the words of C.S. Lewis. I remember this moment like it was today. I know where I was. What I felt. The weather. The song playing on the radio. It is still alive. The song was "Who You Say I Am" by Hillsong

Worship. It was July 18, 2018. My eyes widened with supernatural understanding. I am not sure how I got there, but I was glad it happened. I call this the day I found God. For real. The problem of pain on earth was part of free will. Free will had to exist for perfect love to exist. God wasn't bringing me pain, it was just there, and He was, too, so that I could overcome it. And that was a promise I would cling to. Church wasn't the answer. Jesus was. I was finding my way.

Chapter 40

DERACINATION

After looking at Livvy in Orange County and deciding I wanted to know more, I got more serious about a graduate program. The Christian Counseling one in Florida wasn't an exact fit. It could be a backup plan. I found a program for memory and human development at the University of California, Irvine, and thought maybe the program would include epigenetic psychology, the passing down of memory from generation to generation. No matter what program I found, they all wanted GRE (Graduate Record Examinations) scores. I was terrified to take the GRE. I wasn't a good test-taker, and I was honestly afraid of failing. I avoided the test and looked for graduate programs that didn't require it.

After much searching, the best fit turned out to be UC Irvine after all. So I put on my big-girl pants and began studying for the GRE. The worst-case scenario was that I would fail it. Turns out you can't really fail; you just get a low score. I attended new-student orientations and met with professors and faculty. I was on a high! Could this really be my next step in life? Finally! I studied for the GRE all summer. By fall I had my GRE scheduled and decided I would do my best and not worry too much about the score.

I still had to apply to the program at UC Irvine and write a few entrance essays. The program accepted only twenty students each year, and there were at least two hundred at the orientation. And I was almost twice the age of the other applicants. I felt out of my league but stayed confident and focused on my vow. I needed to find someone to help me refine my entrance essays. I wasn't sure exactly what I should say or what they were looking for. Coincidentally, my stepdaughter was renting a room from a lady who was a dean at my alma mater in its sociology department. Her name was Jodie. She agreed to help edit the papers and guide me in the admission process.

I wrote my two papers: Personal History Statement and Statement of Purpose. Yikes, I was quite overwhelmed with what they hoped to learn about me. I submitted them to Jodie. Jodie's husband, Ruben, was an editor and former university professor. He asked to review the essays, too. After reading mine, Ruben suggested I read a memoir by a local author, Rain of Gold by Victor Villasenor. He thought the story would resonate as Victor Villasenor outlined his family journey over three generations. I took his suggestion and was glad I did. I read the memoir in three days. I could barely put it down.

Ruben also recommended I look up the definition for deracination and asked if I had ever made a connection between my work in human trafficking and my personal history essay. I hadn't. I didn't even understand why he would ask me. Those two things didn't connect for me. He smiled. I looked up deracination. Deracination is the work of uprooting.

Ruben suggested that an internal force was at work in my passion toward human trafficking — a call to heal, to uproot, the family dysfunction through the lives of others. That got my wheels spinning. All the years I spent feeding the homeless, the work I had done with youth and kids in the foster system, my passion for exposing sexual exploitation in San Diego County. I wasn't just interested. I coordinated whole city-wide events for three years to encourage others to get involved in exposing these crimes. I never connected my own family pain to this work. I had pursued these passions long before I was even aware of the family patterns of crimes against humanity.

I had been working all along toward healing something inside me through helping others. Ruben illuminated this story, as I had never seen it before then. Just like the story that I could somehow fix the father I needed by my dating all the guys who lied, who were emotionally unavailable, and who drank. The human story is a powerful one.

With much editing and lots of time and devotion from Jodie and Ruben, I got my essays done. My GRE scores came back, and I was very surprised. I didn't do super well in math (no surprise), but I scored relatively high in writing. The scores were fine for the program. My GPA from my undergraduate work was lower than the university typically accepted, but there wasn't anything I could do about that. I gave my application my all and then waited.

Chapter 41

VOICES

I had just submitted my application for the UC Irvine PhD program. I was relieved to be done studying for the GRE and writing the essays. Vince had just completed his Life Skills class and decided he needed to take it a second time. There was so much to be absorbed. I spent this time reading and rereading Soul Care by Dr. Reimer. I wanted to explore the demon topic more. Besides giving me relief from alcohol, the seminar I had attended piqued my interest in this subject. I had always steered clear of it because, frankly, it scared me.

What I was processing and reading I would share with Vince. He wasn't really enjoying our conversations. He was, frankly, also scared by the demonic stuff. And, unfortunately, the more I shared, the more nightmares he had. I mentioned that maybe he could benefit from looking at the demon issue for himself. He didn't think that was for him. I was still learning and by no means had any answers.

In December 2018 Vince and I were awakened in the middle of the night. My mom was in the house. We both heard her say, "Hello." We sat up. How did my mom get in? Why was my mom here in the middle of the night, in the dark?

Vince got up and put on pants. He went to see what was going on. I rolled over and tried to sleep. He could figure it out. I was tired. Vince walked back into the bedroom and woke me again.

"There is no one here. The house is locked. The lights are off. All the doors are shut. Your mom isn't here," he said, with a deer-in-the-headlights look on his face.

"What are you talking about?" I sat up, now fully awake.

"I am not joking. No one is here," he answered.

"What the heck was that?" Hairs stood up on my neck.

"I have no idea, but now I can't sleep," he said.

The next day Vince got a copy of Soul Care. I had been reading the book for almost a year at that point. Soul Care combined with Life Skills was wreaking emotional and mental havoc on Vince. I can't say I didn't hate that. I felt less alone. Since I had been wading through my own muck and mire for years, it was nice to have company. Vince would read some of the book and then throw it across the room. The chapter on family patterns was especially troubling to him. He would read it for a week and then put it down for weeks at a time.

After Vince had been reading for a few months, I asked him if he wanted to be a guinea pig for the deliverance that was outlined in the back of the book. I wanted to try it and figured it would be safe with some friends as backup at our house. He agreed, maybe reluctantly. We found a few friends willing to come over and try it out with us.

I planned an evening when Livvy would be with my mom. Our friends came over, but Vince was now very hesitant and sat quietly on the couch, almost nonresponsive. I had no idea what I was doing. I was literally reading instructions from the back of the book. We all felt strange and out of our league. As I began, Vince's whole demeanor changed. My friends looked at me with uncertainty. I was supposed to be in charge, but I was wading out too far. I decided that maybe I didn't have enough information to conduct a deliverance session.

"Hey, friend. Are you okay?" I said to Vince, as he sat frozen on the couch.

"Who you callin' friend?" he replied in a raspy voice as he glared at me with eyes I had never seen before.

My friend's husband jumped up and came across the room and stood between Vince and me. He wasn't sure what Vince was going to do because of his response. I stepped back and put the book on the kitchen table, declaring I wasn't going down that road. I wasn't equipped for this type of spiritual encounter. We all agreed. Almost immediately Vince was back to himself. The entire situation freaked him out, though. He decided he would go to the seminar in Florida that Cathy and I had attended.

Vince attended the seminar. That experience is his own story to tell. When he returned, work became a real challenge for him. There was so much in the music industry that he hadn't seen before, or he saw it but had overlooked it. After all, the business is summed up as sex, drugs, and rock 'n' roll. He had a few encounters during his next gigs and told me he had to quit once and for all. I was all for it. He had been in the music industry for eleven years. We were moving into a new season.

In March 2019, I received my letter from UC Irvine. I was not accepted. I was sad. But I also felt hopeful. I took a night job waitressing while Vince stayed home with Livvy, and we began working on plans for what lay ahead for us. Livvy would be five soon and starting kindergarten. We wanted to buy a house, but the California market was out of our league. We started to look at other places to live.

I really loved the house we lived in. We had been there three years, and I didn't want to move away from comfort. But it made sense to find a state we could afford and a neighborhood with a sense of community and a school within walking distance for Livvy. I prayed, but I never felt like I was getting any insight. Where should we move? Should we move? What was next for us? I didn't like working nights. Vince didn't have his day job anymore. There had been so much growth for us, and I liked the comfort we just started having after all those years of chaos. I was starting to feel angry at God again. Wasn't I entitled to a little comfort? Where had God gone? Again, I couldn't discern Him.

Chapter 42

UNCOMFORTABLE

I had grappled with both my fathers' love and rejection and abandonment. Although it felt like a lifelong endeavor, I had made progress. I had noticed patterns and was intentional about healing around the father subject. But in the season of deciding where we should live, I lost hope. I wanted a father to tell me where to go. Actually, I wanted God to tell me where to go. I prayed He would. I cried for answers. The decision felt bigger than me, and I didn't want to make the wrong one.

I would decide: Let's move! The next day I would say: No, let's stay. I did this for weeks. Vince would start looking for houses and jobs in another state, and then I would change my mind. It was maddening for both of us. One day I sat on the couch and looked out the glass slider. Vince sat next to me. I was angry. He asked what was wrong. He knew I was struggling to get direction for our family. He didn't seem to have the same struggle. He was trying to honor what I wanted to do, where I wanted to go. He just wanted me to decide. I didn't want to make a mistake. I wanted God to tell me what to do next.

"You are waiting for God to come in on a white horse and rescue you from making a choice," he said.

"Yes! Yes, I am," I replied in anger.

"God doesn't work like that, you know," he said simply.

"Why? I want to be rescued!" I cried out, then slammed my cup down and began to cry.

I wanted to be rescued, a father to come along and show me how to make good decisions for my family. I wanted reassurance. If God told me what to do, I couldn't mess it up on my own. If I had to make the choice, I would surely be doomed. I had it all wrong. God wanted me to stand up in dignity and make a choice to go where I wanted, where Vince and I wanted to go. To make a choice, and God would be with us. That was it. No magic.

After hours of agony and crying, I said to Vince that I didn't want to be comfortable anymore. If comfort meant sitting back and stopping the growth we had started, I didn't want comfortable. I wanted different. I wanted to shake it up. I asked if he wanted that, too. He did. I said, "Then, let's move. Let's go somewhere we don't know. Where we are forced out of our comfort zone and required to grow through the discomfort." He smiled.

We decided to move to Woodstock, Illinois, where we knew one family. We would live five minutes from my wonderful friend Cathy.

May 2019, we moved across the country. I had been in San Diego for thirty-three years. I had only known 75 and sunny, convenience, and the ocean. I was spoiled. Even though I had challenged myself in the recent years, I hadn't experienced the challenge of being somewhere new like Illinois. Our pastors in San Diego were thrilled that we were moving near Cathy. Cathy and her husband had helped start our church in San Diego many years before. Cathy had recently started a church that met in her home in Illinois, a home church. Our San Diego pastors felt it appropriate that we could now support Cathy in her new church. It was a "pay-it-back" type of thing.

We found a quaint little house, and my parents helped with the down payment. Vince found a job, and I got my Illinois real estate license. There was a local school for Livvy and a cute little town to explore. At first the transition wasn't as difficult as I thought it would be.

Even though God and I had our ups and downs through the years, I thought I was in a good place with Him. Vince and I were doing better than we had in all the years of our marriage, and my parenting was vastly improving. For all intents and purposes, it was a good move.

I had been in church since I could remember, so the thought of a "home church" was slightly uncomfortable. It didn't feel right. I loved Cathy and deeply respected her. But I was thinking she went off the deep end with the home church thing. Only rebels do home church. It was small and intimate and awkward. There was nowhere to hide, you know?

But Vince and I decided to give the home church a try and see what would come of it. After all, we wanted to be uncomfortable, but Cathy had to sell me on the idea. I wanted to know how she came to the decision to quit her job as pastor at the church down the road and do something so drastic. It really felt insane to me. She gave me the names of some authors to read, and I found some podcasts. Cathy held my hand through my questions, and I was actually really shocked by some of the books she recommended. These guys were talking about something called the ecclesia, better known as the fellowship of believers, aka the people who follow Jesus and the faith that teaches that Jesus is God.

That was me. I hadn't bought into the whole religious rigamarole, but I did go to church, because if I believed Jesus was God, that's what you did. Well, when I read through the history of how the church got to where church is, I was astounded. I hadn't known much of church history and how it had become so controlling and wrapped up in human traditions and motivations. Many of these authors were pastors, some of whom had had big churches, who came to change their understanding of their faith. The idea of church then became for them simply a group of people with the same faith gathering to share food, sing, and share their faith and talk about the teachings of Jesus. I could buy into this concept, but home church was still small and uncomfortable.

Chapter 43

FORT WAYNE

A few months after we moved to Illinois, Cathy told me Dr. Rob Reimer, the author of Soul Care, would be over in Fort Wayne, Indiana, in September. I so badly wanted to meet him. I had been reading his book for two years. Cathy and I made plans to go see him.

September seemed to creep up on us quickly, and before I knew it, we were on our drive over to Indiana. I don't recall ever having been in Indiana. The Midwest states are so close together, you can travel to another state in a few hours, unlike California, where you can travel all day and still be in California. Cathy and I talked the whole ride about everything that had been happening — her home church, and Soul Care, and her experience with the deliverance seminar we attended in Florida. Before we knew it, we were in Fort Wayne.

The conference was awesome. I thought I would get to see Dr. Reimer do some deliverance like he had described in his book. But it turned out this wasn't that type of conference. I was kinda bummed out. During the break on the second day, I stirred up courage to introduce myself. My heart was pounding out of my chest, but I had to ask him about my darkness and the connection to my Aunt Alpha's rape and the voices that had terrorized me. I couldn't come all this way and leave without asking him.

I got my question out as quickly as I could. I didn't want to be a bother.

"Do you think we can be connected to our family trauma via memories?" I asked.

He smiled kindly, and I waited for a textbook answer like I had gotten from so many other professionals over the years, something like, "Yeah, we are connected. Makes sense. You're not crazy," that type of thing. But, instead, he answered my question with a question.

"Can I ask you some questions? They will be very direct and personal," he said.

"Sure," I said, not expecting such a question.

"Have you ever sensed a dark presence in your room at night and were unable to move? Some call it sleep paralysis."

"Yes," I replied.

"Have you ever had sexual nightmares that left you feeling dirty and gross?"

"Yes," I replied.

"Have you ever had profane images during your sacred time with Jesus?"

"Yes," I replied, tears now filling my eyes.

"Have you, or anyone in your family, been sexually abused?"

"Yes, to both. Lots of sexual misconduct in my family," I replied behind tears.

"You have demons. I am not doing deliverance at this conference. If you come next month to Ohio, I will make sure to take care of your deliverance," he said.

I nodded and said, "Thank you," turned and walked away to the bathroom, wiping my tears but holding back from fully crying until I could get into a stall.

The break was over, and we were all finding our seats again. The conference resumed, and Dr. Reimer started talking about deliverance. Hmm, I thought, maybe something I said caused him to address this topic.

"I wasn't planning on doing any deliverance at this conference because this isn't a deliverance conference," he said. "But I asked the pastor if I could demonstrate a deliverance today because a lot of you are curious about it." He looked right at me and said, "I was hoping for a volunteer." He nodded at me.

I nodded my head in agreement, and he asked me to come up to the front with him. I was shaking, terrified, and yet so ready for it. I had read his book so many times since Europe. I had even tried to conduct a deliverance with Vince. I was completely intrigued with this topic and had been searching for answers to my darkness and the family dysfunction for so long. I had no idea what to expect except what I had read in his book.

He was the kindest soul you could encounter. It wasn't like the deliverance I had seen growing up where the pastor shouts at the demons and people shake and freak out. Dr. Reimer looked at me and just began to ask questions. He instructed me on what to expect, and the whole room went dark. I didn't see the crowd anymore, I had tunnel vision, and my hearing waned just as it had done at the Florida seminar. But this time Dr. Reimer asked the right questions, and he wasn't shy. He stood in confidence. He had done this thousands of times before. He asked about molestation, sexual abuse, rape, incest, bestiality, child sacrifice, spirits, and many more. He never raised his voice and never let it get out of control. With each set of questions, he asked if a demonic entity was connected, if I answered positively, he would cast it out and continued with more questions

There were moments when my vision went totally blank, like I had gone blind, and I told him I couldn't see anything, and he commanded my sight back, and it came back. There were moments when I could hear only a loud ringing, like I was about to pass out, and he would cause it to stop. I cried through the entire thing, and he was so gracious and kind. He was gentle and never shaming. I had never experienced a single encounter like this in my entire life. I felt so cared for and protected, like Jesus Himself was there. I think He must have been.

When I got back home, I told Vince about the whole thing. And then the most miraculous thing happened. I made love to Vince, and for the first time in my entire life, it was just me and him. There were no voices in my head. No perversion plaguing my mind. No disconnection. No fear. No darkness. I was there. And Vince was there. And that was it. I cried.

Chapter 44

BREAKING THE CURSES

It was a miracle, and I was thankful. But along with it, something new was happening. Because I had disconnected for so long, and participated in the perverted thoughts for as long as I could recall, they didn't vanish completely. They seemed to be creeping back. But I noticed them and could actually shut them off, or I could go back to participating in the disconnect. Now I had a choice. I wondered about this and realized It wasn't the demons influencing me anymore. These patterns of behavior were just habits now, and I could change them. Breaking the habits would be difficult — they were long set — but I was committed to breaking them.

A week or so after my deliverance with Dr. Reimer in Fort Wayne, I had a new connection on my Ancestry.com account. I had joined Ancestry to reach my family, especially the paternal side I hadn't known. But this new connection was on my maternal side, and we shared a lot of cMs, or centimorgans, which show how much DNA you share with someone. Family stories began to pop up in my mind, and I realized this person's story must be the one about the incest baby I had heard about. She must be the daughter of her grandfather.

I decided to message the new connection via the Ancestry app. I introduced myself and gave my mom's information, in case she knew us. She had my mom's maiden name. She had heard of my mom and maybe had met her at one point. Then I asked her if I could intrude with a very personal question. She obliged.

"Is your dad your grandfather?" I messaged.

"Yes. How did you know?" she replied. "I only just found out, and I am on Ancestry to try and connect the dots."

I told her there had been family stories, and I had been doing a lot of research recently on the sexual misconduct of our family. We corresponded for the next few months. I apologized to her on behalf of our ancestors' crimes. She didn't think it was my place to apologize. It didn't matter, I wanted to do it.

Around this time, I found more family — some cousins, on both my maternal and paternal side. I interviewed them about their stories of our ancestors and the family dysfunction. I found out my mom's first cousin had been murdered and had left behind a daughter. I heard about physical and sexual abuse of the boys in the family, too. The crimes weren't just against women.

I decided to research more on family patterns and their effect on the next generations. There was a lot of new science on epigenetics and inherited trauma. I had read some of that already, but I was intrigued mostly by the stuff in the Bible about generational connections to patterns. I understood that when natural laws are broken, it becomes like a curse. Murder, rape, theft, rage, abuse, molestation — when you commit a crime on someone, something happens in the spiritual world. Laws are broken. I finally understood why God would create such rules. He knew that when the laws were broken, they hurt us and spiritually hurt the next generations, making it easier for the next generation to commit the same infractions. Like an open door to a room, inviting the generations to come inside.

I could relate to this; I had been experiencing it. The Bible had a remedy, too. It was called identificational repentance, when the priests would confess and repent for the infractions committed throughout generations of families. I had wondered if I could do this for my family. I decided it would be worth it — hard, but worth it. I wrote each ancestor's name on a piece of paper. Then I scribbled down each thing I knew had happened, a crime or burden or struggle. I did it back three generations, and for each aunt and uncle, great-aunt and great-uncle, too.

I put myself in the shoes of each person, and then I tried to imagine what it was like to be them, in their childhood, in their home with their family. I imagined what was going on in the world at large and in their region. I cultivated as much compassion as I could, and then I imagined them watching me, hoping I would do what they hadn't done while they were on earth, and I offered a deep, heartfelt apology for each offense they had committed. After each one, I would say from my heart, "And I forgive you for this offense and release you."

I can't explain to you the relief and compassion I gleaned from this experience. I was able to let go of so much grief and anger and bitterness. It took months to cover the three generations. I would take Livvy to school and come home and curl up on the floor and cry for hours. The pain was huge.

It was in this process that I decided to reach out to my biological grandfather. Guarded and unsure, I had distanced myself from him ever since I had met him. But my heart was now open to him. I messaged him, hoping he would be open to me. He was. It was a slow start, as it should be. But it was healing.

Chapter 45

FORGIVENESS

Even though Dr. Reimer had already done my deliverance in Fort Wayne, I ended up going to Ohio in October 2019 for his deliverance conference. I just wanted to learn more. I was still processing what had happened and the things my family had struggled with. It was surprising to me that I had been in church my entire life but never seemed to find there the answers to the real terror behind my struggles. But now I was beginning to understand that Jesus was indeed God, and, for the first time in my life, the Bible I had always read now made sense.

There is a lot to unpack with the belief that Jesus was God. I always took it for granted, but it's a huge concept. Jesus was the human form of God, coming to this human population, to pay the price for the corruption Evil had instilled. That is also a big concept, just like the concept in C.S. Lewis's The Problem of Pain that I had understood the year prior — free will had to exist for perfect love to exist. There could be no force or coercion from Love to choose Love, meaning, Evil could have a way into human existence. If there was one human who, using their free will, did not choose Love,

Evil could have influence. God put the system in place knowing He would have to come to humanity as a human to break the power Evil had on humanity. And God did that.

Those concepts I hadn't quite grasped. I was back and forth in asking the question, "Is God good if these heinous things happened to me, to my family?" Why would I struggle so intensely with darkness and wanting to die and the fear that my life was only an accident? After my deliverance, it was like a blindfold had been taken off my eyes, and the demons who had blinded me no longer had influence. I learned that Jesus had told his disciples to conduct deliverances for people once they came to faith. Jesus knew that was the way to see God clearly, to walk without shackles.

I made mention earlier in the book that struggles are real, we can't live without them. They essentially create the opportunity for strength, like lifting weights. But struggles without hope, without support or redemption, create death within. That was what was happening to me. The balance between the two is so essential. Knowing that, I don't want to tuck away the spiritual understanding I have and be content to keep it for myself and fail to pass it forward to the next generation.

In Ohio I sat in the second row. I wanted to watch and see and listen. I wanted to absorb the work. There was a guy in the front row who had been in Fort Wayne. He was also eager to learn more. During the segment on forgiveness, he became increasingly distracting to me.

My mind started playing imaginary conversations with him about getting married. In my imaginary story, I would respond with pretentiousness and flash my wedding ring. This scene played over and over in my mind until it became annoying. Annoying enough that I stopped and asked myself, Okay, what's going on?

I felt God whisper the answer: "You still have issues with rejection and abandonment. You want this guy to pine after you so you can reject him. What you are imagining has nothing to do with this guy or your faithfulness to Vince. It has to do with your fathers. You want them to come beckoning to you so you can reject them. You want retribution!"

My heart crumbled and tears pooled up in my eyes. I did want retribution. I still hadn't let go of getting revenge for the pain I had suffered. Did I even want my fathers' love and attention, or did I just want it so I could reject them? Had I attacked men in this way all my life? I had to forgive my fathers once and for all.

The first night of the conference I checked into my hotel. I was staying alone again, but this time I wasn't full of fear (that was a huge celebration). In place of fear, I had another overwhelming feeling. It was shame, and it was haunting. There was someone else I needed to forgive — myself. Again, I whispered what was this connected to, why was I feeling this shame? A memory came flooding into my mind. A memory of my greatest shame from an act of my own will. A memory I had worked through with Aaron, and told my inner healing pastor, and my best friend, but still never felt it was resolved.

The memory was from when I was twelve, prepubescent, bombarded with perverted thoughts and feelings, which I now know were mostly because of the sexual abuse and family demons. At the time, though, I had no idea why I was struggling and had begun to own the "badness" as my own. My mom had a daycare center. All the kids would take naps in the living room. Since I was homeschooled, I would have quiet time at this time, too. One day I took quiet time in the living room, where all the kids were sleeping, and I ended up in a perverted mind frame. (I now know it was a demon of pedophilia influencing me.) I masturbated on the floor near all the sleeping kids.

Since that day, I have held on to the shame. I couldn't forgive myself. If I did, it meant letting myself off the hook, and if I did that, I would become a pedophile. The shame convicted me and held me prisoner, keeping me from feeling free.

Others in my family had also been influenced by these demons and had acted out this pattern. But I wanted freedom, not shame. This was no longer a demon issue; it was a forgiveness issue. I would not become a pedophile if I let go of the shame.

I took a piece of paper and wrote the whole story of my shame. I cried over it. I cried for the little girl who was locked in a prison of toxic patterns. I saw my little self with huge rusty chains dug into the skin of my back. I looked to see where the chains went. They pulled me down and went back as far as I could see. I removed the chains with the help of Jesus. My tears and His tears were the salve for my skin where the chains had been. I took myself off the hook that night. I tore up the paper with the story and put piles of the torn paper in each of the four corners of the room. I said, "Now it is done."

Chapter 46

DELIVERANCE

Ohio was so great for me. I was on a high. The last day of the conference Dr. Reimer did deliverance for anyone who wanted it. The line of those wanting it went down the center of the room and out the door. I sat in the front, eyes wide with amazement. Every once in a while, there would be a story like my own, and I would tear up. Jesus was tangible. Love flowed through the entire room. Compassion and dignity. When we came to the last few hours, Dr. Reimer looked at me.

"You good?" he asked.

"Yes. I just want to learn as much as I can," I replied.

"You wanna come up and help me?" he asked. "You can take notes. By this time, I start to get tired, and if I forget where I am in my prayer, you can help me."

Did I want to! I flew to my feet and grabbed a pen and notebook. I went straight up and leaned on the podium and took notes for each person he prayed for. I was in pure nirvana.

Listening to and watching these deliverances, I thought of how I was so acquainted with death or suicide in many places in my life. I thought of the demons of death or suicide in my own family. I hadn't realized how many people in my family had been murdered. Also, when sexual abuse is prevalent in a family, it, too, often causes the desire to flee or escape or die. When David died, I literally wanted to die, too. I thought also about how demons are sometimes shared with people closely connected to one another or to the places where you live, like the demons of darkness at the red house and all the people who had died there, including the one who had committed suicide. Dr. Reimer had evicted the demons of death and suicide during my deliverance in Fort Wayne.

When the conference was over, I asked Dr. Reimer if he could do a deliverance for Vince. He said to come to New York in December and he would be sure to do deliverance for Vince. We booked tickets for December.

As promised, Dr. Reimer did Vince's deliverance. I sat with eyes wide once again. I realized our marriage was growing. We both were finding freedom for ourselves, and we were paving a path for Livvy to have a healthier life.

The end of this conference was like the one in Ohio, except this time Dr. Reimer had other people facilitate deliverance, and he roamed the room to help where needed. I heard him call to me with the microphone.

"Bethany, lead a group. Vince can help you," he said.

Lead a what? I had never done that! I wanted to do it. How could I not? I jumped in the deep end that day, and Vince and I walked ten people through deliverance. My heart was alive. I had so much to learn, and still do, but I had been invited to walk into a bigger space. A space where freedom was blooming. I wanted to walk into it. I wanted to invite others into it, too!

When I talk to other people doing similar soul processing, we seem to agree that a space opens in the spiritual realm when we start to heal. For example, when I started doing my inner healing work and reading Soul Care for the first time, it seemed to allow me to function more easily without hesitation. I could confront topics that formerly paralyzed me with fear. Then, when I had my first deliverance, there seemed to be a chain reaction in my family, as if the spiritual darkness I was experiencing was a chain connected to others in my family. When it broke from me, it loosened its grip on the others who were connected to the chain.

The space phenomenon is hard to explain, but I feel it exists. There isn't any hard research on the topic. It is either a coincidence or a chain reaction. When I prayed for my past generations and brought their struggles to God, it seemed to open space for other family members to heal. I would hear stories about other family members noticing things in the family dysfunction they hadn't noticed before. Some people even started down the path of greater healing or had energy and time for the process they hadn't had before.

Something like an invitation presents itself to people in our families when we start down this road, as if Jesus is saying to them, "You're invited to heal this pain, too." Not everyone accepts the invitation, but some do. I believe if I commit to the healing, going into each dark room of the family legacy, bringing the junk in the trunk to Jesus, the more I can heal, and the greater opportunity they have to heal, too. No doubt we are all connected. I was handed the invitation, too.

For me, finding my way and breaking the legacy of brokenness came through the answers the power Jesus provided. It's strange how I got lost in the church growing up, wanting freedom and chasing modalities that might shed light on the demonic struggle. Sadly, the church I had placed my hope in had itself gotten lost in religion and rules. Luckily for me, I found Jesus, who had been there all along.

...Still finding my way

Epilogue

There are handfuls of other stories that have come to light in my family, but there are two I want to highlight. I also want to share a small portion of my paternal side of the family that connects with my legacy of brokenness.

In the last few years, I had the opportunity to live with my Nana, the same one who told me the Aunt Alpha story in the beginning of this book. In helping her organize her filing cabinet one day, I came across an old letter dated 1980. I asked if I could read it, as it was from her Aunt Helen. The letter contained the information that Nana was conceived during an affair her mother had. Her step-dad loved her and raised her as his own. They never acknowledged the infidelity. Her bio-father never knew her. But, Aunt Helen knew Nana was conceived by two people secretly deeply in love. Nana was what Aunt Helen called, a child made in love. I couldn't believe it!

This feeling of not belonging started way before my birth. Nana had never known her biological father! I asked Nana about the legitimacy of the news. She believed it wasn't true. But there was one hang-up: We had all done Ancestry.com tests in helping me explore the family DNA. It so happens that none of us who did the DNA test, including Nana, was connected to the father who raised her. Instead, we were connected to another family, a family sharing high amounts of cMs with us. A family we didn't know. This family happened to share the same last name as the man mentioned in the letter from Aunt Helen.

After much exploring, we connected with the family, and stories aligned. There were not any direct relatives still alive to consent to a DNA test to confirm Nana's biological father 100 percent, but we narrowed it down to two people in their family based on age, location, and names.

Nana went her entire life telling stories about how she longed for her father's affection and never quite got it. It was the feeling of not belonging pattern, happening well before I came along. It was deep-seated. I went for a walk to try to adjust my mind to this newfound information about my heritage. Tears fell from my eyes. I remembered the moment I had found out about my biological father. I remember subsequent experiences around meeting him, my family's backlash, and many other situations that had caused grief.

Nana never knew her biological father; she was conceived during a love affair. She never knew the truth. There is no shame in this story. It is history. It is where I came from. It is part of me. I shine a light on the darkness to expose it to the truth. In the light of truth, darkness loses its grip. I am freer having known the truth.

Days after I found out about Nana, I decided I would tell my mom and sisters. We had a trip planned to celebrate my parents' fortieth wedding anniversary in Montana. I planned to tell my mom and sisters around the dinner table, thirty years after I found out I had been adopted that night around the campfire on my parents' tenth wedding anniversary. This time my mom would find out that her grandfather wasn't her biological grandfather.

The news went over almost as badly as the news about my adoption thirty years before. My sisters were not pleased, and after they excused themselves, my parents sat with me in silence. My mom was stunned, her mind reeling with thoughts. Since my mom was noticeably upset, I asked how she was feeling. She expressed grief and confusion.

"Imagine how I felt hearing my dad wasn't my biological father," I said. I had to say it. I had to share the pain about my adoption that they had never validated. They had always downplayed my feelings and the fact that my biological father had significance in my life. She connected! I could see it in her eyes. The pain and confusion she felt was one step removed; the news was about her grandfather. My news had been about my father, one step closer. But in that moment, I felt her apology for causing me to feel invalidated for all those years. It was sincere for the first time in my life. It was balm to my heart and a healing I had needed for so long.

The second story picks up one year after my deliverance in 2019, in the midst of the COVID pandemic. I received an e-mail from a cousin. The e-mail was sent to the entire family, making a confession of harm toward another family member many years before. I immediately called the person who had been hurt to see how they felt about the e-mail, but they had not read it yet. So, instead of discussing the e-mail, we examined the intricacies of pedophilia and the research we both had been doing.

I wondered at the time if my cousin's e-mail confession had come about as a result of some of the work I had been doing in the spiritual arena. The space had opened. I do know that I had been asking questions about the family years prior to illuminating my own darkness. I was sharing what I was learning, and sometimes that was very difficult. Because of what I had learned around the sexual crimes within my family, I was doing all I could to illuminate the darkness around us. It was only because of the work I had completed with the inner healing pastor that I was able to discourse with other cousins about the sexual abuse in our family. I could discuss it without becoming paralyzed with fear. I hoped, somehow, these discussions had impacted my cousin's process toward admitting his guilt and confessing to the family in his e-mail.

It's important to note here that confession in itself is not the end result. There is more work to do. Many professionals agree that admitting to yourself your own wrongdoing is the first step. I believe, though, that confessing to others is courageous, especially when it's a sexual infraction. The cousin who sent the e-mail had been working toward rehabilitation and had faced several natural consequences for his actions. I know there is more work to be done with this situation and with our family dynamics around this topic.

It may be a tough road to navigate, but I am willing. I want to be the one who raises her hand to join the conversation. I understand some of our family feel this topic is too overwhelming, exposing, and shameful. To me, it is healing to speak of it, to search for solutions. I want to understand. I want to be part of the answer and involved in healing our future. It didn't start with us.

The legacy of brokenness needs first to be seen, then illuminated, and finally banished into the darkness where it belongs. Then healing can begin. It is possible to heal the legacy of brokenness.

Almost every example I used in this memoir was from my maternal side because this book was written to that side of my family. But for greater clarity, I wanted to summarize the paternal side of my biological family, which was also wracked with similar abuse, disconnect, and rage. It has only been by the grace of God that I have deepened my relationship with my paternal grandpa. At the time of this writing, my paternal grandpa is eighty-six years old. Four months ago, he moved twenty minutes from my house. This alone is a blessing, since I only met him in my twenties and never connected with him until after my first deliverance in 2019. We have grown so close, and I have been able to hear and learn so much about life, spirituality, and my family.

I learned that *his* mother, my great-grandma, had been raped by her father when she was eight years old. His mother, trying to protect her younger sisters, became hypervigilant. Nevertheless, her younger sister married very young and was subsequently shot dead by their physically abusive brother-in-law. It was a double homicide. She and her husband both died that night. (Her husband was my great-grandfather's brother, so I lost two ancestors to murder on the same night.) My great-grandma grieved not being able to save her sister from death. Because of the rape by her father and the murder of her sister by her brother-in-law, my great-grandma became a man-hater, affecting my grandpa's upbringing.

My grandfather struggled to connect to women, and just a few years after having children (my biological father was his first child), Grandpa and Grandma divorced. Grandma quickly went out and married a severely toxic man who infused our family with rape and sexual abuse. Grandma had exhibited her own symptoms of being sexually abused by leaving home and dropping out of school. Bound by harsh religion and fear, she betrayed and manipulated her own children. This was the home my biological father grew up in. It is no wonder my biological father fled when my mom got pregnant. I do not excuse his absence in my life, or his fear reaction, but I do understand with a compassionate heart. I've had to grieve my parents' divorce and the loss of my biological father. To be honest, it is a large wound, and I have to process deeper layers of grief on occasion.

Deliverance Recap

    You may be asking how do I know this stuff worked. It's been four years since my first deliverance with Dr. Reimer. I've had subsequent sessions over the years. Each new session covered new levels of struggles. I know it worked because the effects have been lasting. I am integrating wholeness.

    What I mean by integrating wholeness: There are less fractured parts of myself. I have minimal negative thoughts and reactions, and I have zero panic. I can walk through the dark without fear. I sleep soundly at night with Livvy sleeping on the other side of the house in her own room. I don't get plagued by perverted thoughts or imaginations anymore. I have sex with my husband without being terrorized by the family demons of rape and rage and perversion. The effects have so drastically changed my life that I have begun aiding other people in the care of their soul, and I help people through their own spiritual deliverance. That is my truest testament — being able to help others without spiraling into the abyss myself. I know my own work is not finished, but every day I celebrate the freedom I have found.

    A little about the difference between the soul and the spirit. I believe humans are tri-part beings: **We are a spirit, have a soul, and occupy a body.** Each aspect of us needs to be attended to. We cannot merely care for our body and not attend to our soul and spirit. Some people opt to focus on only their spirit and forget their body and soul.

I define the **soul** as mind, wants, feelings. The soul often gets overlooked in religious circles. However, it is not God's job to attend to the care of our soul; it is ours. Caring for our soul is a big, continuous job. It's the job of humans. The soul is where we think, feel, and behave based on our past experiences. This is where trigger reactions occur, reactions that come from pain. If our soul is out of whack or wounded, we operate from a place of fear, confusion, anxiety, or depression. If our soul is in pain, we disconnect and struggle with intimacy or relationship issues. It is harder to be a partner, parent, employee, or a friend when our soul struggles. If our soul struggles, we tend to lose ourselves, become enmeshed with others, and are unable to properly own our sovereignty, identity, or possess confidence at our core. Only we, as adults, can own the responsibility for the care of our soul. No one else can fix this for us.

Our **spirit** is our essence. It is the part that lives on after our body ends. I do not attend a corporate church, nor do I consider myself religious. But I am a follower of the Christian faith, and I do believe Jesus was God. I am devoted to studying the Bible and engage in spiritual practices such as prayer, worship, and meditation, among other practices. These practices only grow my faith; they don't make my faith. I believe the human spirit is secure with God once one chooses the faith that Jesus was God. There are no more deeds or works to do for spiritual security. God as Jesus did the heavy lifting at the cross. Though spiritual disciplines can deepen faith, no disciplines can earn security. Don't take my word for it; you can find out for yourself. I tried to earn my freedom and found out Jesus was my answer all along, just not the way the corporate church had been teaching me. As you have just read, not only did I have faith that Jesus was God, but I used the tools Jesus provided to get rid of the darkness causing the immense fear within me. I was able to apply the instructions of Jesus to liberate my spirit of the demons that plagued my life and caused hopelessness.

Our **body** manifests the conditions of our spirit and soul. What I mean is that if we have bitterness, rage, fear, envy, arrogance, hate, intimidation, pride, shame, and more, our body can manifest symptoms of this negativity. Symptoms can include heart issues, depression, anxiety, autoimmune disorders, chronic pain, skin disorders, brain disorders, mental diseases, and more. Do I believe that every physical condition is a symptom of the soul or spirit? No. I do believe our bodies can exhibit physical struggles based on other factors. However, let's not attribute every physical thing to biological or physiological factors. Consider issues in your emotions, your thoughts, and your spirit — even your inherited brokenness — and how they might be impacting your physical body

In our stories we find our history and learn we are all connected. Go after your story. The world is waiting for your shackles to come off. To watch you soar. To be inspired!

"What we don't know is already killing us."

Dr. Rob Reimer

Special Thanks

To my family for allowing me to share our story to honor and bring light to the patterns that bind us. My hope is in the freedom.

To my parents, who, by all means, did the best they could to raise me within the legacy of brokenness.

To my grandpa, Will Barkley, who has unashamedly shared story-after-story with me to help me process the paternal side of the family.

To my Nana, who graciously allowed me to use her story to connect to my own.

To Wendy, my cover designer and dear friend.
www.pinkolivedesign.com

Thank you, Jackie Logue, for doing amazing work on editing my book, The Roadie Wife, Finding My Way – Book II.

To Cathy, my pastor, mentor, and friend — grandma to Livvy Lou — for always holding space for me through my trials and questioning.

To Dr. Rob Reimer for his dedicated work toward renewal and the care of the soul. Your work has forever changed my life. **www.renewalinternational.com**

For Vince, my dearest husband: Your support in my chaos and turbulence is more than any wife could ask for. As I write and process, you always give the space, and an embrace, as needed.

For Livvy Lou, my Peaceful Warrior: Because of you, I pursued greater freedom and walk with hope. May you be all you were designed to be, free of encumbrances.

"Creativity embeds knowledge so that it can become practice. We move what we're learning from our heads to our hearts through our hands. We are born makers, and creativity is the ultimate act of integration – it is how we fold our experiences into our being...
The Asaro tribe of Indonesia and Papua New Guinea has a beautiful saying:
"Knowledge is only a rumor until it lives in the muscle."

Brene Brown
Rising Strong